# Innovative Business Strategies

The book explores how technology is transforming business operations and organizational management. To thrive in the digital world, companies need to be flexible, forward-thinking, and above all, human-centered. The book examines four key areas for attaining these goals:

- Traditional management approaches are insufficient in today's digital landscape. Companies must adopt innovative management models incorporating artificial intelligence, big data, and digital platforms to maintain competitiveness. These technologies enable process automation and data-driven decision-making, though implementation faces challenges including high costs and resistance to change.
- Sustainable innovation is a strategic necessity rather than a voluntary action. This dual-externality innovation type requires balancing environmental protection with enterprise competitiveness, demanding both internal management changes and external stakeholder engagement.
- Corporate finance should evolve beyond traditional profit optimization, incorporating digitization, sustainability, and decision psychology. Modern financial management requires adaptability to dynamic market conditions while considering broader strategic implications.
- Humanoid robots are a growing presence in enterprises. There should be a focus on human-centric, ethical implementation approaches that augment rather than replace human capabilities while addressing privacy, bias, and accountability concerns.

Business management today is as much about understanding technology as it is about making thoughtful and ethically sound choices. This book shows a way for organizations to remain effective by building strategies based on clarity, responsibility, and respect for the people involved, both within and outside the organization.

# Innovative Business Strategies

## In the Era of Digital Transformation

Judyta Kabus, Joanna Antczak,
Ida Skubis, and Monika Zajkowska

Routledge
Taylor & Francis Group
NEW YORK AND LONDON

Designed cover image: Shutterstock

First published 2026
by Routledge
605 Third Avenue, New York, NY 10158

and by Routledge
4 Park Square, Milton Park, Abingdon, Oxon, OX14 4RN

*Routledge is an imprint of the Taylor & Francis Group, an informa business*



ISBN: 978-1-041-23432-6 (hbk)
ISBN: 978-1-041-23960-4 (pbk)
ISBN: 978-1-003-73936-4 (ebk)

DOI: 10.1201/9781003739364

Typeset in ITC Garamond Std
by SPi Technologies India Pvt Ltd (Straive)

# Contents

# About the Authors

**Dr Judyta Kabus** is Assistant Professor at Jan Długosz University in Częstochowa. She is Doctor of Humanities and Doctor of Management and Quality Sciences, and President of the Częstochowa Region Women's Association. In 2023, she was awarded the Bronze Medal of the President of the Republic of Poland for Long Service. She is Member of the Committee on Organisation and Management Sciences at the Polish Academy of Sciences. She is an Expert at the National Centre for Research and Development and the National Agency for Academic Exchange.

Dr Kabus is an author and co-author of over 100 scientific publications, as well as a reviewer of scientific papers in Polish and foreign journals. She is an author of teaching materials for learning German and education for the development of scientific research. She is responsible for the organization of national and international conferences and is a multiple-time winner of the Rector's Award of the Częstochowa University of Technology. Dr Kabus is a long-term scientific collaborator of VSB in Ostrava, a participant in the Erasmus+ student exchange programme, a member of the TNOiK Scientific Society, and a manager and member of several international projects.

Her work focuses on innovation, social responsibility, sustainable development, green economy, market trends, and urban logistics.

**Dr Joanna Antczak** has a PhD in economics and is a research and teaching assistant professor at the Jarosław Dąbrowski Military University of Technology in Warsaw.

Her research and publication achievements include the management of an economic unit in a changing environment, including financial management; controlling its application in the enterprise and economic and defense security of the state, including cybersecurity; and the use of tools such as financial analysis, models for assessing the risk of bankruptcy of enterprises, and cost analysis. She gained her professional experience working in financial institutions and accounting offices. She participates in conferences and expert panels in the field of methods, including assessing and forecasting the economic and financial condition of enterprises, expenditures on cybersecurity, and corporate finance management.

**Dr Ida Skubis** is an assistant professor at the Silesian University of Technology in Poland, within the Department of Organisation and Management. She holds a PhD in linguistics and possesses master's degrees in four languages—English, German, French, and Spanish—and speaks five languages, with Polish as her native language.

Dr Skubis has extensive professional experience in both academia and business, having held managerial positions (Manager, Director, PR Manager, and Director of the Hotel) in international companies and lived in various countries, including Spain, Greece, France, and Austria. She currently serves as the CEO of the Housing Community.

Throughout her career, Dr Skubis has been awarded numerous scholarships and fellowships, including those in Germany, Austria, France, the Czech Republic, Turkey, Bosnia and Herzegovina, and Poland. She is actively involved in interdisciplinary AI projects and frequently participates in international conferences. Additionally, she serves as a reviewer for international journals on AI-related topics.

Dr. Skubis has received numerous scholarships and awards for her scientific research, including a prestigious scholarship in France under the Marie Skłodowska-Curie Actions (Horizon Europe) for her research on the Ethics of AI.

She received the scholarship of the Minister of Education and Science for Outstanding Young Scientists, granted for three years for academic achievements. A record number of 1,711 applications were received in the 2025 competition, and only 228 scientists were awarded this scholarship. From the social sciences, 44 awards were granted all over Poland, and only four scholarships were given in the discipline of management, and Dr Skubis is among those four people.

**Dr Eng. Monika Zajkowska** is Assistant Professor at the Warsaw School of Economics, College of Management and Finance, Institute of Management, Department of Sustainable Business. She conducts didactic classes and a seminar on the topics of innovation management, R&D projects, open innovation, sustainable innovation, human resource management, project team management, organizational behavior, knowledge management, consumer involvement in the development of new products, and cooperation in innovations. She is the President of the Management Board of the Hanseatic Institute for Supporting Small and Medium Enterprises, and an expert in the evaluation of innovative projects at the National Center for Research and Development (R&D), Digital Poland Project Center, Ministry of Regional Funds and Policy, Ministry of Development, and Polish Agency for Enterprise Development. She is also a member of many institutions associated with the SME community, including the Hanseatic Parliament—the largest institution associating small- and medium-sized enterprises in the Baltic Sea Region.

# Introduction

The modern business world is experiencing a profound change, characterized by digitalization, technological innovation, and evolving economic and social dynamics. Today's organizations operate under the conditions defined by constant technological change, global connectivity, and the explosive growth of data and artificial intelligence. In this fast-moving context, the ability to adapt, innovate, and manage resources strategically is more essential than ever for maintaining competitiveness and achieving sustainable growth.

*Innovative Business Strategies* examines how companies are responding to the challenges and opportunities brought by digital transformation. It considers how new technologies are influencing management practices, organizational structures, financial decision-making, and the integration of tools like artificial intelligence and humanoid robotics into business operations. Through a broad yet detailed perspective, the book explores how digitalization is redefining business models, shaping decision-making, and raising important ethical and regulatory questions.

At the core of the digital revolution is the power of businesses to handle and make sense of immense amounts of information with remarkable speed and accuracy. Digital technologies have become vital not only for making internal processes more efficient but also for driving innovation, deepening customer relationships, and creating entirely new business models. Yet alongside these opportunities come significant challenges—from cybersecurity threats and technological disruptions to the complex task of leading organizations through continuous change.

The progress of the modern global economy is based on the use of digital technologies to process, store, and transmit information. Technology plays an important role in shaping the competitive potential of both countries and economic units. Businesses face numerous challenges in the digital age.

They operate in a fundamentally different way compared to traditional business models. Digitalization is changing the way organizations conduct their operations, communicate with customers, manage data, and make decisions. Businesses need to be flexible, open to innovation, and ready to adapt to a rapidly changing business environment. This requires constant monitoring of technological advances and proactive adaptation to new digital trends and solutions.

Changing market conditions in which an economic entity operates require its executives to choose management support tools, particularly in the area of locating the company's "bottlenecks." Knowledge of the financial situation of an economic entity becomes indispensable in making decisions at both operational and strategic levels. Maintaining the company's solvency is an extremely important element for its existence, both in the short and long term.

This volume addresses management issues in the face of the dynamic development of technology and digitalization. It discusses how companies should adapt their strategies and structures to a changing business environment where technology plays a key role.

Chapter 1 analyzes the importance of innovative management models in the context of digital development and digital transformation. It points out that modern models integrating advanced technologies and flexible organizational structures are key to effective management in a dynamic environment.

It discusses the role of innovation in adapting to changing market conditions and highlights challenges such as investment costs, resistance to change, and technological risks. It argues that innovative approaches enable organizations to optimize operations, build competitive advantage, and achieve long-term strategic goals.

Chapter 2 elaborates on the problem of developing and introducing sustainable innovations in a digital environment. In order to keep up with the pace of change, modern enterprises are forced to intensify their efforts to adopt digital innovation paths. This challenge becomes even greater when considering innovations based on sustainable development, which seek to balance economic, environmental, and social factors. The aim of this chapter is to determine the use of technological trends and the advisability of using digital technologies in the innovative activities of enterprises, with particular emphasis on innovations based on sustainable development. The issue is analyzed through the prism of three overarching current technological trends: Intelligent, digital, and networked solutions as the basis for successful business activities in the digital era. It identifies different approaches to defining the determinants and conditions for the development of sustainable innovations. It also identifies challenges in analyzing the positive and negative aspects of digital tools in the development of sustainable innovation.

Chapter 3 analyzes the importance of financial management as one of the most important dimensions in both current and long-term management of a company's operations. Attention is paid to the determinants of financial management of enterprises in the context of their functioning in cyberspace, which is characterized by the lack of borders, dynamism, and anonymity. It discusses the role and application of selected tools used in corporate financial management. Examples of tools based on artificial intelligence that are used in corporate financial management are provided.

Chapter 4 offers an exploration of the increasing presence and influence of humanoid robots in diverse enterprise settings, including tourism, hospitality, gastronomy, healthcare, and corporate management. It examines how these robots, designed to mimic human appearance and behavior, are being integrated into front-line services, administrative operations, rehabilitation, and even executive leadership. The chapter highlights not only their functional versatility and potential to address workforce shortages, improve efficiency, and enhance customer experience, but also the societal, managerial, and ethical challenges accompanying their deployment. With a strong emphasis on autonomy, human-robot interaction, and decision-making, this chapter situates humanoid robots within broader regulatory and ethical frameworks, particularly those defined by the European Union's AI Act and GDPR.

Through critical analysis and real-world case studies, Chapter 4 highlights the importance of a human-centric approach to robotic innovation—one that safeguards human oversight, ensures transparency, and promotes fairness in algorithmic processes. It discusses customer perceptions, trust, and user acceptance, as well as the ethical dilemmas posed by automation in sectors traditionally reliant on emotional intelligence and human interaction. Ultimately, this chapter calls for responsible usage of humanoid robots in enterprises, balancing technological advancement with societal values, regulatory obligations, and the preservation of human agency.

This work offers a comprehensive study of how digital transformation is influencing business management. Written in accessible language and grounded in current research and practice, it provides practical examples to help readers engage with and apply the concepts discussed.

# Chapter 1

# Innovative Business Management Models in Cyberspace

## 1.1 Introduction

Digital transformation has significantly affected almost every aspect of modern businesses. These transformations go beyond technology alone to include changes in organizational culture, as well as the way we manage and build relationships with customers and business partners. Cyberspace has become a key area for companies, offering them the opportunity to introduce new solutions, optimize processes, and reach customers around the world (Wasilewski 2017). However, managing in this environment requires models that integrate advanced technologies with innovative business practices (Szpringer 2012). Only such an approach makes it possible to create added value, effectively manage customer relationships, and build a sustainable competitive advantage.

Today's businesses are operating in an increasingly complex environment, in which dynamic technological and social changes pose new challenges (Brzozowska & Kabus 2018).

DOI: 10.1201/9781003739364-1

Globalization, the rise of digital technologies, and increasing customer expectations are forcing organizations to constantly adapt their strategies and operating models (Zajda & Vissing 2024). Under such conditions, innovative management models are becoming an essential element of success. They enable companies not only to effectively exploit the potential of cyberspace but also to respond quickly to market changes, better manage resources, and develop more flexible organizational structures.

Cyber governance is a process that involves planning, organizing, motivating, and controlling resources to achieve strategic organizational goals in a digital environment (Koibichuk et al. 2021). It requires a new approach to managing data, security, and customer and supplier relationships. Cyberspace, being a space for global information exchange, presents companies with both opportunities and challenges. Organizations must confront cybersecurity threats, manage data in accordance with current regulations, and develop competencies to operate effectively in a dynamic online environment.

Innovative management models allow organizations to leverage the potential of the digital environment to achieve market competitiveness (Hausschildt & Salomo 2011). By integrating modern technologies into management practices, companies can streamline their processes, increase efficiency, and build lasting relationships with stakeholders. At the same time, operating in a digital environment requires not only the implementation of technology, but also a profound change in management thinking. This means developing flexible organizational structures that are able to respond quickly to changing market conditions, and promoting an organizational culture based on innovation and continuous improvement (Czakon 2015).

This chapter examines selected management models that combine modern technologies with the need to adapt to a changing environment. Its purpose is to show how innovative approaches can help companies meet the challenges of today's economy, as well as how to effectively use the potential of cyberspace to build a competitive advantage. In particular, issues related to management in the online environment, such as cybersecurity, data management, process optimization, as well as building relationships with customers and suppliers, will be discussed. In a dynamically changing business environment, the ability to effectively manage in cyberspace is becoming crucial for the survival and growth of modern organizations. This chapter attempts to comprehensively present innovative management models that meet the needs of businesses in the era of digital transformation.

## 1.2 The Concept of Innovation in the Field of Business Management

Innovation in business management is a key element in building competitive advantage in a rapidly changing market environment. The term, although often used as a synonym for modernity or originality, actually covers a much broader range of activities and processes. The etymology of the word "innovation" comes from Latin (innovare), meaning "to renew" (Kopaliński 1985). In the scientific literature, innovation is defined as activities leading to the introduction of new or significantly improved products, processes, strategies, or organizational structures, which aim to increase the efficiency and added value of an enterprise (Grudzewski & Hejduk 2000).

Joseph Schumpeter, considered a pioneer of innovation research, was the first to introduce the broad concept of innovation into the economic dictionary in 1911. He defined it as a process involving (Schumpeter 1912):

- Introducing a new method of production: Schumpeter pointed to changes in the technology and organization of production that enable higher efficiency. New methods can include automation, the use of new materials, or innovative approaches to managing the production process.
- Reorganization of the method already in place: Innovation can consist of optimizing existing processes, which brings tangible benefits without the need to introduce completely new technologies.
- Opening a new market: Exploring new markets for existing products or services is a key element of innovation. In this way, companies can increase their competitiveness and access to new customer segments.
- Improving an existing product or producing a new one: Product innovation is one of the most visible manifestations of technological progress.

Contemporary definitions show innovation as a process, take into account a wide range of activities and values, and emphasize its importance for different levels of functioning of organizations and communities:

- **Lee, Olson, and Trimi** view innovation as any attractive idea, new opportunity, or approach that can be applied in a variety of ways to create positive value for an organization, community, or the general welfare of humanity. According to this concept, innovation is a dynamic process involving creativity and implementation (Lee et al. 2012).
- **Myers and Marquis** point out that innovation is a complex process that starts with an idea or new concept and ends with a solution that brings tangible economic and social benefits. Innovation can involve both products and processes, while also being a tool for adapting to changing market conditions (Myers & Marquis 1969).

- **Schippers, West, and Dawson** recognize that innovation is the intentional presentation and application to teamwork, organizations, or work groups of new ideas, processes, products, or procedures that are intended to produce benefits. Innovation encompasses not only creativity but also the practical implementation of the results of that creativity to achieve profits or improve efficiency. Highlighted values of contemporary definitions (Schippers et al. 2015).
- **Kotler** argues that innovation is a process involving the creation, verification, development, and implementation of ideas aimed at profit (Kotler 1999).
- **Griffin** emphasizes the organization's efforts in developing new products and services and improving existing solutions (Griffin 1996).
- **The Oslo International Manual** defines innovation as the implementation of new or significantly improved products, processes, marketing, or organizational methods. The key element is the transition from idea to practical application (Oslo Manual 2008).

Contemporary definitions of innovation, especially in the context of enterprises, emphasize its multidimensional nature and its key role in building competitive advantage and the long-term success of organizations (Drucker 1992; Rojek 2014). Innovation in enterprises focuses on creating both economic and strategic value (Hausschildt & Salomo 2011). Economic value is expressed in improving the efficiency of processes, reducing costs, increasing revenues, or capturing new markets (Janasz & Kozioł 2007). At the same time, companies can use innovation to build an image of being socially responsible, offering solutions that improve the quality of life for customers, support sustainability, or address important social challenges. Innovation in companies is a process (Grudzewski & Hejduk 2000) that requires a strategic approach. They begin with idea generation based on an analysis of market trends, consumer needs, or technological capabilities (Rogers 2003). Then, companies move on to vet the ideas, assessing their viability and potential impact on the organization. The next step is to implement the solution, which often requires the involvement of interdisciplinary teams and effective change management (Litfin 2000). An important final step is to monitor the effects of the implemented innovation, which allows for assessing its impact on the functioning of the company and possible further improvements (Białoń 2010).

Scalability is another important aspect of business innovation. Solutions that can be implemented on a large scale give companies the opportunity to grow dynamically and expand their operations. Scalable innovations allow companies to increase production, enter new geographic markets, or offer products and services to more customers. This allows companies to effectively increase their market share and generate higher profits. An important distinguishing feature of corporate innovation is the integration of creativity with practicality (Baruk 2012). New solutions must not only stand out for their originality, but also respond to the real needs of the market and customers. With this approach, companies are able to create products, services, or processes that are both innovative and functional, which translates into their market success. Innovation is thus becoming a key tool that enables companies to adapt to changing market conditions, build customer loyalty, and increase their competitiveness. In this way, companies not only achieve economic benefits but also shape their position as leaders in selected industries.

Thus, the typology of innovations in the enterprise is broad and includes, among others, product, process, organizational, and marketing innovations (Żukowska & Pindelski 2010) (Table 1.1).

Product innovation refers to the introduction of new products or services to the market that better meet customer needs.

**Table 1.1 Types of Innovation in the Enterprise**

| *Type of Innovation* | *Description* | *Example* |
|---|---|---|
| Product | Introduction of new or improved products/services to the market. | New car model with advanced autonomous technology. |
| Process | Changes in production processes or work organization, improving efficiency, and reducing costs. | Automation of production lines in the factory. |
| Organizational | Reorganization of company structure or management methods. | Introducing hybrid work in the organization. |
| Marketing | Innovative promotional and distribution strategies. | Use of personalized campaigns in social media. |
| Social | Changes that lead to improvements in social conditions or relationships within an organization. | CSR programs to support the local community. |

*Source:* Own elaboration.

Process innovations, on the other hand, involve technological improvements and the optimization of manufacturing and operational processes, leading to lower costs and greater efficiency. Organizational innovations focus on structural changes and new management methods, such as the implementation of digital tools or the reorganization of teamwork, while marketing innovations include the development of new promotional strategies, the implementation of innovative sales models, and better alignment of offerings with market expectations (Mendling & Brocke 2018).

Today's businesses face many challenges related to globalization, rapid technological change, and rising customer expectations. Under such conditions, innovation is becoming an indispensable part of survival and growth strategies. Companies must constantly introduce new products, improve their production processes, reduce costs, and develop effective marketing methods to maintain their position in the market (Reformat 2017). The innovation management process involves several key stages: Identifying market needs, generating ideas, testing new solutions, implementing, and monitoring results (Rojek 2014). A key role in this process is played by leaders who motivate teams, minimize resistance to change, and foster an innovative culture within the organization (Figure 1.1) (Pomykalski 2001).

Figure 1.1 shows a diagram of the innovation process, which includes five key stages. Each stage describes specific actions that organizations can take to successfully implement innovation. The process is flexible and can be adapted to

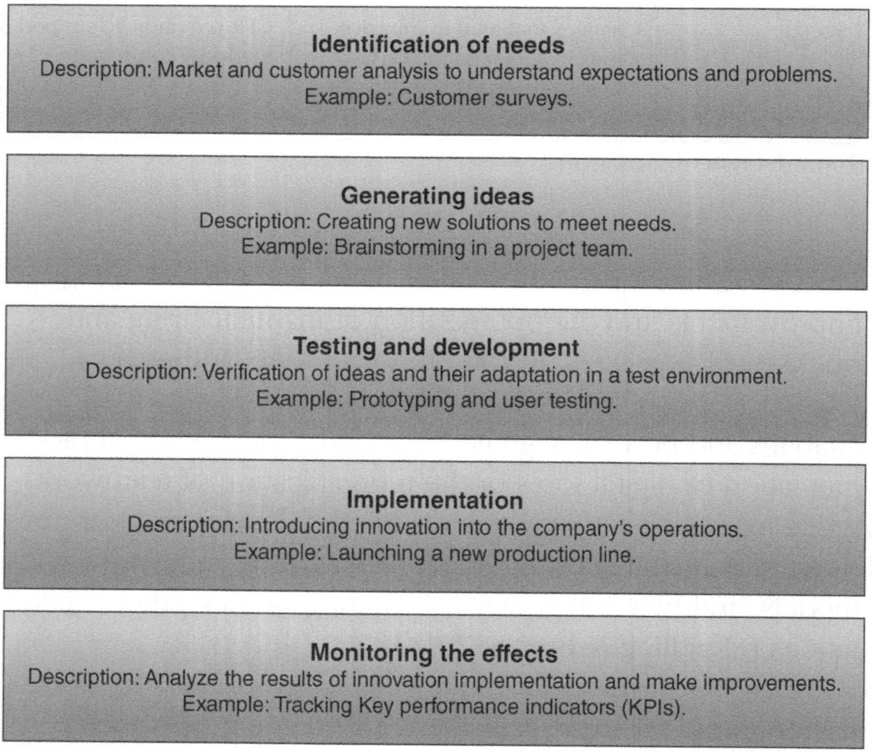


**Figure 1.1 Implementation of innovations.**

*Source:* Own elaboration.

different needs and company specifics. The outline presented can be applied to a variety of industries and organizational environments. Each step requires involvement of project teams, data analysis, and openness to change. By applying the presented steps, companies can effectively innovate, gaining a competitive advantage and generating value for customers.

Innovation brings numerous benefits, such as increased competitiveness, improved operational efficiency, increased customer satisfaction, and long-term business growth (Table 1.2).

Through innovation, it is possible to introduce modern technologies, create new business models, or adapt to changing market conditions. Despite the numerous benefits, the implementation of innovations is also associated with high risks and significant financial outlays (Gallo 2010). Developing new technologies, designing products, or restructuring processes requires investments that do not always guarantee

**Table 1.2 Benefits of Implementing Innovation in a Company**

| *Area* | *Benefit* | *Example* |
|---|---|---|
| Production | Reduce costs and increase product quality. | Use of new technologies in production, such as robotization. |
| Marketing | Better matching of offerings to customer needs. | Personalizing e-commerce offers based on data analytics. |
| Operational efficiency | Improving internal processes within the organization. | Implementation of an ERP system in an enterprise. |
| Employee development | Increase team commitment and competence through training and development programs. | Organization of creative workshops for the team. |
| Market position | Building competitive advantages and capturing new markets. | Introduce innovative services, such as product subscriptions. |

*Source:* Own elaboration.

immediate returns. The main challenges associated with innovation include (Hausschildt & Salomo 2011):

- Financial risk: Uncertainty about whether investments in new solutions will yield the expected benefits.
- Organizational resistance: Introducing change may be met with reluctance from employees or other stakeholders.
- Short-term disruption: A change in strategy or processes can lead to temporary disorganization in a company.

In conclusion, innovation in business management is not only a response to modern economic challenges but also a tool for creating value and building competitive advantage. Organizations that effectively manage innovation are able not only to survive in a dynamic market but also to set new directions of development and set standards in their industries. Innovation is the foundation for success in today's knowledge- and technology-based economy.

## 1.3 Innovative Business Management Models

Innovative business management models are a fundamental element of the strategy of modern organizations (Grudzewski & Hejduk 2000), which operate in an environment of dynamic technological change, globalization, and rising customer expectations (Olavarrieta & Villena 2014). They enable companies not only to adapt to changing market conditions but also to proactively shape the future by creating new values and strategies (Szuszkiewicz et al. 2024).

Today's business management models take into account many key aspects, such as the use of modern technology, integration of internal and external processes, sustainability, and personalization of offerings. This allows organizations to better respond to customer needs, while increasing their operational efficiency and building a competitive advantage.

Innovative management approaches allow companies to flexibly adapt their operations to changes in the environment, including new market requirements and social and technological trends (Janulek 2022). The introduction of elements such as artificial intelligence, the Internet of Things (IoT), big data, or blockchain allows organizations not only to automate processes but also to optimize the use of resources, better forecast trends, and make data-driven decisions (Kreiterling 2023).

Moreover, modern business models emphasize building collaborative ecosystems with diverse partners, customers, and suppliers. By creating comprehensive value networks, organizations can increase their ability to innovate and introduce products and services that respond to changing market expectations (Belenzon & Berkovitz 2010).

The basis for successful implementation of innovative management models is a strategic approach that takes into account factors such as the development of employee competencies, knowledge management, and the building of an organizational culture based on openness, cooperation, and continuous improvement (Belenzon & Berkovitz 2010). Companies that successfully implement innovative management models become leaders of change in their industries, while increasing their resilience to the challenges of a dynamic business environment.

Thus, innovative business management models not only support adaptation to changing market conditions but also enable organizations to anticipate and shape future trends, which is becoming a key factor for success in a global and complex business environment (Jabłoński 2013).

A business model defines how an organization operates, including how it generates value, builds customer relationships, leverages resources, and achieves profitability

(Bis 2013). Innovative versions incorporate modern technologies, sustainability, and collaboration within business ecosystems (Holm et al. 2013). A key feature of such models is their flexibility, interdisciplinarity, and future orientation.

Innovative business models are characterized by the ability to dynamically adapt to the changing market environment, enabling organizations not only to adapt but also to set new standards in their industries. By integrating advanced technologies, they can automate processes, personalize their offerings, and make better use of available data. As a result, companies can respond more effectively to customer needs while increasing their operational efficiency (Guerrero et al. 2021).

Sustainability is a key element of today's business models, which increasingly incorporate measures that minimize negative environmental impacts while promoting social responsibility. Pursuing sustainability not only improves a company's image but also increases the loyalty of customers, who are increasingly guided by environmental and social values when making purchasing decisions (Li et al. 2020).

Today's business models also include ecosystem collaboration, linking companies, partners, suppliers, and customers into integrated value networks. Such collaboration enables the creation of more comprehensive and personalized solutions that meet the needs of different stakeholders, as well as fostering innovation through knowledge and resource sharing (Ostrovska et al. 2021).

In addition, features such as modularity and scalability of innovative business models are of key importance in business models. Thanks to them, organizations can effectively develop their business by adapting individual elements of the model to the specifics of local markets, industries, or customer preferences (Wisniewski 2017). In this way, companies can flexibly implement changes and quickly respond to new market opportunities or threats (Table 1.3).

A business model can also be understood as a formal analytical tool that supports the work of improving an

**Table 1.3 Features of Business Innovation Models**

| *Features* | |
|---|---|
| Value proposition | Offering unique benefits beyond the product or service, while also taking into account social and environmental aspects. |
| Customer segmentation | Using advanced analytical tools to accurately identify audience needs. |
| Value delivery channels | Development of digital and e-commerce platforms to effectively reach customers. |
| Customer relations | Building long-term, interactive relationships using CRM technology. |
| Revenue streams | Diversify revenue streams, such as subscription or pay-per-use models. |

*Source*: Own elaboration.

organization by extracting the relevant elements of reality and the relationships between them (Scuotto et al. 2023). It consists of such elements as people, tasks, technologies, and structure (Table 1.4).

A model is also a picture of reality that takes into account relevant variables and relationships between elements, allowing these variables to be manipulated for analysis and decision-making (Kuczera 2013).

The construction of models involves their normative nature as well as the possibility of comparing them with the results of empirical studies. As a result, models help to accurately determine long-term plans for the operation of the enterprise, identify problems, and design and implement optimal solutions. A model can be considered a hypothetical mental construction, which is a simplified picture of a fragment of reality, in which the relevant elements are extracted due to the purpose of analysis (Szpringer 2008). A model, whether a construction, diagram, or description, shows the operation, structure, features, and relationships of a phenomenon occurring in an enterprise. It can be defined from two perspectives (Wielgos et al. 2021):

**Table 1.4 Main Elements of the Business Model**

| *Elements of the Model* | |
|---|---|
| People | Employees, customers, partners, and stakeholders who participate in organizational processes. People are a key resource influencing innovation, organizational culture, and the execution of the company's strategy. |
| Tasks | Activities undertaken to achieve an organization's goals. Include operational, management, and support processes that are relevant to value generation. |
| Technologies | Tools and systems used for process automation, data analysis, communication, and innovation. Technology plays a key role in increasing efficiency and competitiveness. |
| Structure | Organizational structure or the way a company is organized in terms of roles, responsibilities, and information flows. Structure affects the flexibility, scalability, and efficiency of an organization. |

*Source:* Own elaboration.

1. Structural Approach: Treats a model as a construct that reflects reality through simplification or idealization. In this view, a model is a tool that allows one to analyze the key elements of an organization and identify the links between them.
2. Functional Approach: Views the model as a tool that replaces the real object in cognitive operations and experiments. It performs the functions of reflection, abstraction, communication, and control, and supports experimental research. It allows for analyzing various action scenarios, avoiding the cost of actual experimentation.

Models allow companies not only to better understand the business environment but also to forecast the effects of innovation. Through their use, companies can accurately identify problems, analyze available solutions, and design optimal operating strategies.

It can be seen from the above that the model serves as a versatile tool that finds application in both research analysis and strategic management processes. Its primary function is to support the organization in defining problems by identifying their causes, determining the goals to be achieved as a result of the solution, and predicting the effects on the business of the enterprise. The model also makes it possible to develop and compare different options for action, allowing the organization to select the most optimal solution (Szpringer 2008). The process ends with the implementation of the selected scenario and monitoring of its effects to ensure the optimization of processes and the effectiveness of implemented actions (Figure 1.2).

The business model is a key tool in an organization's strategic planning, enabling companies to effectively manage their resources and achieve their long-term goals. Through its use, companies can determine exactly what resources and competencies are needed to achieve their desired results, allowing them to more precisely allocate available resources and develop the skills that bring the greatest value to the organization.

One of the important aspects of a business model is its ability to identify potential directions for expansion, both geographically and with respect to new customer groups or market segments (Sobińska 2014). By analyzing the model's structure and performance, a company can identify market niches that are underserved and assess which products or services can best meet their needs. This allows companies to develop their business in a sustainable and thoughtful manner, minimizing the risks associated with entering new markets.

The business model also supports the building of competitive advantages, which is particularly important in a dynamically changing business environment (Georgellis et al. 2000). By integrating modern technologies, such as artificial intelligence, big data analytics, and process automation, companies

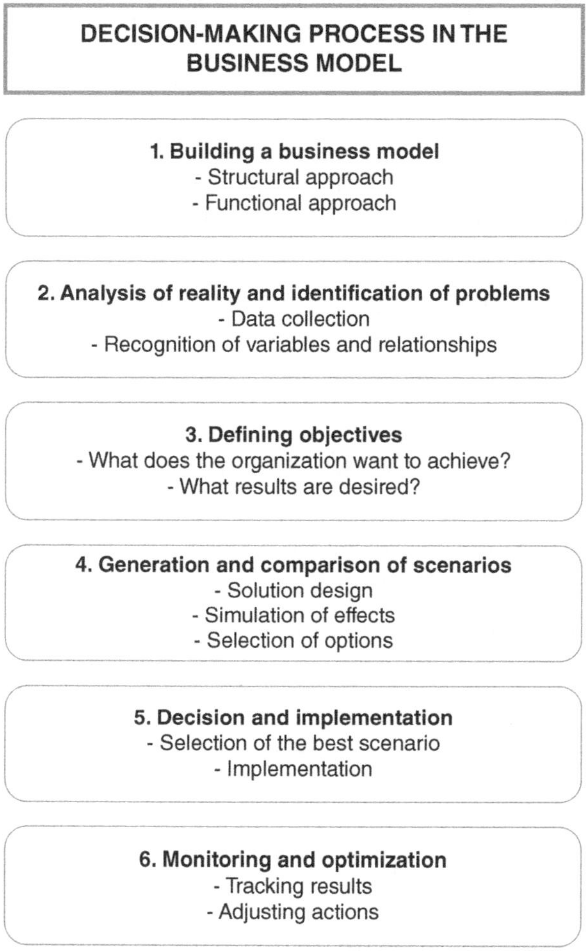


**Figure 1.2 The decision-making process in a business model.**

*Source:* Own elaboration.

can increase the efficiency of their operations and offer more personalized and innovative solutions to customers (Sobińska 2016). At the same time, incorporating the principles of sustainability into the structure of the model allows the implementation of activities that not only bring financial benefits but also strengthen the positive image of the company as a responsible business partner and participant in local communities (Broccardo et al. 2023).

In this way, the business model becomes not only an operational tool but also a strategic compass that allows the organization to successfully navigate the complex market environment, respond to challenges, and take advantage of opportunities (Baruk 2012).

In addition, the model can be viewed as a hypothetical mental construct that represents a simplified view of reality. It takes into account only the key elements relevant to the objectives of the analysis, which makes it a practical and effective tool. As a result, the model makes it possible to solve complex problems in a structured manner and to design strategic actions tailored to the specific needs and challenges of the organization. Its application contributes to a better understanding of business phenomena and supports decision-making in a dynamic and complex market environment (Wisniewski 2017).

Modern business management models combine traditional approaches with innovative solutions to effectively respond to the dynamically changing needs of the market and customers. As a result, organizations are able not only to meet their operational goals but also to shape strategies that create sustainable enterprise value (Hameed et al. 2021). The value proposition in modern business models is much more comprehensive than in traditional approaches. It encompasses unique benefits delivered to customers that go beyond the mere products or services focused on in traditional models. Innovative models take into account emotional, social, and environmental aspects (Olifirov et al. 2019). Companies are increasingly focusing on building deeper connections with customers, offering solutions that are not only functional but also contribute to positive experiences and meet social responsibility needs (Yopan et al. 2022). The organizational structure of modern business models is characterized by a modular approach to process design. Modularity enables companies to flexibly adapt their operations to market changes, allowing them to quickly introduce new products, services, or technologies. As a result, companies are able to respond effectively to customer needs and adapt to new conditions, while minimizing the risks associated with overly complex internal structures. Modularity involves dividing activities into independent but cooperating modules or units that can be easily changed, expanded, or replaced without affecting the overall system. In practice, modularity means that an organization does not have to rebuild its entire structure in response to new challenges, such as technological changes, customer needs, or market fluctuations. For example, a company can introduce a new product, service, or technology into its business model by integrating it as a separate module without having to modify existing processes. Likewise, if a module is no longer effective, it can be quickly replaced by another or adapted to meet current requirements (Machado et al. 2024).

Modularity is particularly important in a dynamic business environment because it allows organizations to:

- Experiment with new solutions: The modular structure allows new strategies or products to be tested on a limited scale before full implementation.
- Scale the business: Individual modules can be easily duplicated or expanded, which is useful for expanding into new markets or serving more customers.
- Enable personalization: Modules can be customized to meet the specific needs of different customer groups, allowing more personalized solutions to be offered.
- Respond to change: Modularity enables rapid adaptation to changing conditions, for example, by introducing new technologies or abandoning outdated processes.

In an organizational context, modularity also works at the level of team and project management. Companies can create dedicated teams or units for specific tasks that are separate from the rest of the organization, but work with other modules to achieve common goals. This allows organizations to make better use of their resources, avoid conflicts between departments, and implement changes faster in response to new market needs. Modularity in modern business models is, therefore, not only a feature of organizational structure but also a strategic approach that allows companies to be flexible, innovative, and efficient in managing complex business processes.

One of the pillars of innovative management models is the use of technology. The introduction of tools such as artificial intelligence, big data, and the Internet of Things (IoT) allows processes to be automated, to improve operational efficiency, and to optimize resource utilization. **Automating processes** through technology allows time-consuming manual activities to be replaced by automated systems, which not only increases operational efficiency but also significantly reduces costs.

The use of artificial intelligence and automation tools in areas such as production, customer service, and logistics allows for greater efficiency and better quality of operations performed.

**Personalization of offerings** has become possible thanks to data analysis, which allows companies to better understand customer needs.

**Big data** makes it possible not only to analyze customers' past behavior but also to forecast their future needs, making it possible to provide products and services perfectly tailored to individual preferences (Butryn & Hauke 2018).

Technologies such as **blockchain** increase transparency and security, especially in supply chains. The ability to track the flow of goods in real time and ensure the immutability of data in blockchain systems builds trust with both customers and business partners. Transparency and security are key values today, especially in industries where regulatory compliance and data protection are a priority (Wodnicka 2021).

**IoT** plays an important role in managing resources and making operational decisions in real time. Enterprises use the data generated by IoT devices to monitor their resources, allowing them to react quickly to any changes or irregularities. This approach significantly increases an organization's flexibility and enables effective risk management (Haaker et al. 2021).

Technology also supports decision-making processes by providing advanced analytical tools that identify trends, forecast future events, and minimize business risks. With data analytics that uses statistical techniques, machine learning algorithms, and artificial intelligence to predict future events, that is, with predictive analytics, businesses can make better strategic decisions that not only take into account current market conditions, but also anticipate potential challenges and opportunities (Lee et al. 2012). As a result, technology is becoming not only an operational tool but also a strategic support that allows organizations to build competitive advantage and dynamically adapt to changing market realities.

Incorporating modern technological solutions into business models strengthens innovation, flexibility, and the ability of companies to deliver value to their customers, making technology an integral part of today's management strategies.

The implementation of innovative business models brings with it a number of challenges that companies must overcome in order to successfully implement new management approaches (Visnjic et al. 2016). One of the most important problems is the high investment costs associated with purchasing modern technologies and developing the competencies of teams. Organizations must allocate significant resources to purchase advanced software, IT infrastructure, or process automation (Ngo & O'Cass 2013). Additionally, it is crucial to invest in training employees to enable them to use new tools and technologies effectively. Particularly in small and medium-sized companies, where budgets are limited, this challenge can be a significant barrier to innovating (Lestari et al. 2020).

The second major challenge is the organization's resistance to change. Transforming business models requires not only the introduction of new processes or technologies but also a change in organizational culture, which is often entrenched in existing practices (Li et al. 2020). Employees and managers may be reluctant to embrace new solutions, especially if they involve changing roles, responsibilities, or ways of working (Adrodegari & Saccani 2017). Adapting an organization to innovative models therefore requires not only effective communication but also a commitment from leaders to build trust and convince teams of the benefits of transformation. Another challenge is the technological risk posed by the dynamic development of tools and the need to constantly update them (Stornelli et al. 2021). Technology is evolving at a rapid pace, which means that solutions that are state-of-the-art today may become obsolete in the near future. Organizations need to constantly monitor technology trends in order to invest in tools that have the prospect of long-term use. These risks also include the possibility of failing to implement technologies that do not meet business expectations or are ill-suited to an organization's specific needs (Ober 2022). In addition to these barriers, companies also face the issue of integrating new solutions with existing systems and processes. In many cases, implementing innovative models requires infrastructure upgrades, which can be a complicated and time-consuming process (Salehi & Sadeq Alanbari 2024). It is also necessary to ensure data security, especially when implementing technologies such as IoT or blockchain, which generate and process large amounts of information.

In summary, the implementation of innovative business models is a process that requires significant financial resources, transformation of organizational culture, and continuous monitoring of technology. However, organizations that can effectively manage these challenges gain the opportunity to achieve a competitive advantage, improve efficiency, and adapt to a dynamic business environment.

## 1.4 Analysis of Innovative Management Models in an Innovative Organization

An innovative organization is an entity that is distinguished by its ability to create new value through the introduction of unique solutions, adaptation to changing market conditions, and the use of advanced technologies. In today's economy, characterized by the rapid pace of technological change, globalization, and increasing competition, innovation is becoming a key element in building competitive advantage. Such organizations not only respond to change but also create it, actively participating in the transformation of their industries. Change is easiest to implement in this type of enterprise, as they are inherently open to innovation and constant adaptation to dynamic market conditions. Innovative organizations are characterized by a flexible structure that makes it possible to implement new solutions quickly and efficiently. Their work culture is based on experimentation, testing, and learning from experience, which makes change appear as a natural and necessary part of development.

These companies not only implement new management models but also actively create them, adapting them to their unique needs and goals. Examples include agile management methods, such as Agile or Lean Management, which are often created precisely in innovation environments. These organizations combine modern approaches with traditional practices to create hybrid management systems that increase operational efficiency, improve collaboration within teams, and allow them to better respond to market needs.

By being open to change and experimenting with new management models, innovative companies not only adapt quickly to new conditions but also become transformational leaders, setting the course for other organizations in their industry. This makes them key players in today's knowledge and innovation economy.

One of the management models based on innovative change, implemented in innovative organizations, is the business model using digital technology platforms (CPTs), which plays a key role in economic transformation. In the era of digitization, CPTs enable companies to adapt to dynamic market changes, optimize processes, and create new revenue streams. Key aspects of this model are as follows (Bartczak 2023; Doligalski & Goliński, 2024; Koszany & Jakubowiec 2022):

1. Co-creating value with consumers. Digital platforms allow customers to actively participate in the creation of products and services, fostering an engaged community around the brand and personalizing offers. Examples include:
   a. Kickstarter: It is one of the most popular crowdfunding platforms, enabling creators and entrepreneurs to raise funds for innovative projects. With the support of the community, they can fund products even before they are officially launched.
   b. TripAdvisor: The online review system allows users to rate hotels, restaurants, and tourist attractions. Businesses can adjust their services according to customer reviews, which thereby affects the quality of service and competitiveness in the market.
   c. Yelp: A service that allows customers to share reviews of local businesses and services. Restaurants and other businesses can use customer reviews to improve their services and build loyalty.
   d. Loyalty programs: Companies such as Starbucks and Amazon Prime personalize offers to customers based on their purchase history, which increases engagement and frequency of use.
2. Another aspect of CPT-based models is the development of new revenue streams. CPTs enable the implementation

of modern monetization strategies, such as subscription models, freemium, or digital advertising. This allows companies to diversify revenues, test new business models, and optimize operating costs. Examples include:

a. Subscription models: Companies offering services on a monthly or annual subscription basis generate stable revenues and build customer loyalty. An example is Netflix, which offers ongoing access to a catalog of content instead of traditional sales of individual movies.
b. Freemium model: This involves providing a basic version of the service for free, and users must pay for additional features. Spotify follows this model, offering a free account with ads and a premium version with no restrictions.
c. Digital advertising: Many platforms monetize user traffic through ads. Google Ads uses analysis of user data to deliver personalized ad content, increasing its effectiveness and revenue for companies.

3. Increased scalability is also an advantage of CPT-based models. With digital technology platforms, companies can expand into new markets without investing in infrastructure. They have the ability to enter new markets immediately with a scalable digital infrastructure. Companies can reach customers around the world, avoiding the costs associated with a physical presence in a given market. Examples include:

a. Amazon's global e-commerce expansion has enabled the company to enter markets without opening traditional stores. Thanks to developed logistics and cloud technology (AWS), Amazon effectively reaches customers around the world.
b. Airbnb, a platform based on the sharing economy model, allows individuals to rent properties without owning a large hotel chain. With its digital

infrastructure, Airbnb operates in hundreds of countries without owning its own properties.
   c. Uber, a ride-hailing app, allows drivers to earn money and passengers to use transportation services without the need for their own fleet of vehicles. The scalability of the model has allowed Uber to expand to hundreds of cities around the world in a short period of time.
4. Building network effects, enabled by CPT-based models, increases the number of interactions and user-generated content, which makes platforms more valuable (Abbas et al. 2021; Shree et al. 2021). Companies with network effects are harder to drive out of the market because their value increases as the number of users increases, they gain strength, and are harder to replace with competing solutions (Rohn et al. 2021; Cartwright et al. 2021). Examples of the network effect are as follows:
   a. Facebook: The more users use the platform, the greater the network value. Each new user increases community engagement, which attracts advertisers.
   b. LinkedIn: Growth in the number of users increases the potential of professional networks, enabling better matching of jobs and candidates.
   c. Amazon Marketplace: More sellers are attracting more buyers, fueling the platform's growth.
   d. Google: The search engine's popularity increases the effectiveness of its algorithms and attracts advertisers, which, in turn, funds the further development of Google's ecosystem of services.

A management model based on digital technology platforms is the key to success in the modern digital economy. With CPT, companies can co-create value with customers, develop new revenue streams, rapidly scale their operations, and build strong network effects. Digital transformation is becoming not just a trend, but a necessity for companies looking to gain a competitive edge in a rapidly changing market. In summary, digital technology platforms are the foundation of innovative business models. They enable co-creation of value with consumers, open up new revenue streams, increase business scalability, and benefit from network effects. Thanks to these features, organizations that successfully implement CPT achieve significant competitive advantages and play a key role in transforming the economy.

Artificial intelligence (AI) is revolutionizing the way companies analyze data, make decisions, and interact with customers. The introduction of machine learning algorithms and advanced analytics allows for significant improvements in many areas of business. AI is improving operational efficiency, enhancing customer experience, and optimizing business strategies (Prasanth et al. 2023). AI enables deep analysis of customer behavior and preferences, allowing products and services to be tailored to the individual needs of customers.

AI-based systems can:

- Analyze purchase history and user habits, providing personalized recommendations.
- Segment customers based on their activities, preferences, and demographics, which allows you to better tailor your offerings.
- Automate marketing campaigns by dynamically adjusting advertising content and promotional offers.
- Optimize user experience in applications and websites by personalizing the interface and content.

As a result, customers receive better-tailored proposals, which increases customer satisfaction, loyalty, and purchase conversion.

AI systems also take over many routine and time-consuming tasks, enabling companies to save resources and time. Automated processes include: Customer service, inventory management, streamlining HR processes, or supporting financial analysis of businesses, for example:

- Chatbots and virtual assistants provide 24/7 support, answering users' questions and solving common problems.
- AI systems analyze demand, predict demand, and optimize inventory levels, minimizing waste.
- AI helps recruitment by analyzing resumes, predicting top candidates, and automating employee performance evaluations.
- Artificial intelligence automates invoicing, detects financial fraud, and analyzes expenses. This allows for more efficient budget management.

By using AI, employees can focus on more strategic and creative tasks, which increases innovation and productivity in companies.

Artificial intelligence makes it possible to process huge amounts of data in a short period of time, identifying trends and patterns to support decision-making. AI forecasts market changes, allowing companies to adjust sales and marketing strategies. AI algorithms analyze market data, competition, and demand to dynamically adjust prices for products and services, easily detecting anomalies by identifying anomalies in financial data, website traffic, or customer behavior to respond faster to potential threats. Finally, intelligent analytics systems provide data-driven recommendations to support managers in making key business decisions.

Already today, artificial intelligence is being applied in many sectors of the economy, among others (Vijai & Wisetsri 2021):

- Commerce and e-commerce—personalizing offers, automating customer service, and optimizing the supply chain.
- Medicine and healthcare—disease diagnosis, medical image analysis, surgical robots, and personalized therapy.
- Finance—fraud detection, investment risk analysis, and banking process automation.

- Production and logistics—optimization of production processes, automated warehouse management systems, and robotization of production lines.
- Education—smart learning systems, student performance analysis, and personalized educational materials.

Artificial intelligence (AI) brings numerous benefits, but it also comes with challenges that require attention and appropriate solutions.

One of the key issues is ethics and privacy. With the increasing use of AI comes the need to protect personal data and ensure the transparency and fairness of decision-making algorithms. It is important that AI-based systems operate in a fair manner, eliminating potential biases and undesirable social consequences (Ruiz-Real et al. 2021).

Security is another important aspect of AI development. AI-based systems can become a target for cyber attacks or a tool for data manipulation. Therefore, it is necessary to implement effective protection mechanisms to ensure reliability and resilience to threats.

AI's impact on the labor market presents another challenge. Automation of processes can lead to changes in the workforce, forcing employees to adapt to new technologies. It becomes crucial to educate and develop digital competencies to enable people to function effectively in the changing work environment. The right approach to these challenges will maximize the benefits of AI while minimizing potential risks and negative social impacts. The future of AI promises to further develop intelligent systems that will be even more autonomous, precise, and integrated into everyday life. Companies investing in AI can look forward to competitive advantages and innovative growth opportunities.

Artificial intelligence is no longer just a technological curiosity, but a key tool for digital transformation. Harnessing its potential can significantly improve business operations and open up new prospects for the future.

Virtual reality (VR) and augmented reality (AR) technologies are gaining prominence in marketing and sales strategies, offering innovative ways to engage customers and improve their shopping experience. Companies are increasingly turning to these solutions to make their offerings more attractive, increase consumer engagement, and enhance the quality of service. One of the most popular applications of VR and AR is virtual fitting rooms, which allow customers to test clothes, glasses, or cosmetics in a digital environment. This makes online shopping more convenient and allows customers to better match products to their needs, minimizing the risk of wrong choices. This not only increases shoppers' satisfaction but also reduces the number of returns, which is an important factor for online retailers. Another area where immersive technologies play a key role is in interactive product presentations. With augmented reality, consumers can see how a piece of furniture will look in their home before they make a purchase, or check the functionality of an electronic device without having to visit a stationary store. Such solutions not only increase the attractiveness of the offer but also help build greater trust in the brand (Egieya et al. 2023).

VR and AR technologies are also finding applications in training and education. Companies are using them for realistic training simulations that allow employees to be practically prepared for real-world professional challenges. In industries such as medicine, aviation, and manufacturing, where precision and practical skills play a key role, training in a virtual environment can significantly enhance learning (Kumar et al. 2021).

With the development of immersive technologies, more and more industries are recognizing their potential. Innovative solutions based on VR and AR not only raise the level of interaction with customers but also help companies stand out in the market and adapt to changing consumer expectations. As technology advances and implementation costs fall, their role in sales, marketing, and education is expected to continue to grow (Jayadatta 2024).

Many companies in various industries are successfully implementing virtual reality (VR) and augmented reality (AR) technologies in their marketing and sales strategies, creating innovative and engaging experiences for customers.

For example, Valentino Beauty launched a pop-up in New York with a smart mirror that allowed customers to virtually try on new lipstick shades. This interactive installation attracted about 1,500 people over two days and helped boost product sales.

Shiseido, a Japanese cosmetics company, created an immersive experience in the form of a 360-degree capsule that transported users on a virtual journey to the mountains of Japan, combining visual and olfactory experiences. This innovative presentation was designed to educate customers about the Future Solution LX product line.

Gucci remains at the forefront of innovation, integrating VR and AR technologies into its marketing efforts. The brand has introduced various virtual activations that engage customers in an interactive way, strengthening its position in the market (digitalagencynetwork.com).

Hugo Boss organized a virtual "Planet Hugo" experience on the Roblox platform, promoting its denim collections in an interactive online environment. This initiative allowed the brand to reach a younger audience and increase customer engagement.

Versace introduced virtual Mercury sneakers in the game Fortnite and on the Snapchat platform, allowing users to interact with the products in the virtual world. This strategy combined fashion and gaming, attracting new customers and increasing brand awareness (voguebusiness.com).

In Poland, we are also seeing growing interest in VR and AR technologies in business. An example is Merck, which has used VR for marketing purposes, creating immersive experiences for its customers (gdcvault.com, epicvr.pl).

These examples show how diverse brands around the world are using immersive technologies to create innovative and engaging experiences for their customers, thereby increasing their competitiveness in the marketplace.

## References

Abbas, U., Islam, K. A., Hussain, S., Baqir, M., & Muhammad, N. (2021). Impact of brand image on customer loyalty with the mediating role of customer satisfaction and brand awareness. *International Journal of Marketing Research Innovation*, 5(1), 1–15.

Adrodegari, F., & Saccani, N. (2017). Business models for the service transformation of industrial firms. *The Service Industries Journal*, 37(1), 57–83.

Bartczak, K. (2023). *Modele biznesu oparte na cyfrowych platformach technologicznych*. Difin sp. z oo.

Baruk, J. (2012). Model racjonalnego przebiegu procesu innowacyjnego opartego na wiedzy. *Przegląd Organizacji*, 5, 15.

Belenzon, S., & Berkovitz, T. (2010). Innovation in business groups. *Management Science*, 56(3), 519–535.

Białoń, L. (2010). Zarządzanie działalnością innowacyjną. *Zarys problematyki. Zarządzanie. Teoria i Praktyka*, 1(1), 23–33.

Bis, J. (2013). *Innowacyjny model biznesowy–sposób na zwiększenie przewagi konkurencyjnej. Modele biznesowe*. Łódź: Wydawnictwo Społecznej Akademii Nauk w Łodzi.

Broccardo, L., Truant, E., & Dana, L. P. (2023). The interlink between digitalization, sustainability, and performance: An Italian context. *Journal of Business Research*, 158, 113621.

Brzozowska, A., & Kabus, J. (2018). *Determinants of enterprises' innovativeness in the light of empirical studies–case studies of Austria and Poland*. Zeszyty Naukowe. Organizacja i Zarządzanie/Politechnika Śląska, Gliwice.

Butryn, B., & Hauke, K. (2018). Big data w globalizacji procesów biznesowych. *Informatyka Ekonomiczna*, 1(47), 32–42.

Cartwright, S., Liu, H., & Raddats, C. (2021). Strategic use of social media within business-to-business (B2B) marketing: A systematic literature review. *Industrial Marketing Management*, 97, 35–58.

Czakon, W. (2015). Sieci międzyorganizacyjne w naukach o zarządzaniu–w kierunku sieciowych modeli biznesu. *Studia Ekonomiczne*, 217, 9–18.

Doligalski, T., & Goliński, M. (2024). Platformy cyfrowe. Model biznesu, zastosowania, użytkownicy.

Drucker P. (1992). *Innowacje i przedsiębiorczość*. Warszawa: Wydawnictwo PWE.

Egieya, Z. E., Ewuga, S. K., Omotosho, A., Adegbite, A. O., & Oriekhoe, O. I. (2023). A review of sustainable entrepreneurship practices and their impact on long-term business viability. *World Journal of Advanced Research and Reviews*, 20(3), 1283–1292.

Gallo, C. (2010). *The Innovation Secrets of Steve Jobs*. New York: McGraw Hill.

Georgellis, Y., Joyce, P., & Woods, A. (2000). Entrepreneurial action, innovation and business performance: the small independent business. *Journal of Small Business and Enterprise Development*, 7(1), 7–17.

Griffin, R.W. (1996). *Podstawy zarządzania organizacjami*. Warszawa: PWN, 646.

Grudzewski, W., & Hejduk, I. (2000). Rozwój i implementacja organizacji inteligentnej. *Przedsiębiorstwo przyszłości*, Grudzewski, W., Hejduk, I., (red.), Warszawa: Wydawnictwo Difin, 139.

Guerrero, M., Santamaría-Velasco, C. A., & Mahto, R. (2021). Intermediaries and social entrepreneurship identity: Implications for business model innovation. *International Journal of Entrepreneurial Behavior & Research*, 27(2), 520–546.

Haaker, T., Ly, P. T. M., Nguyen-Thanh, N., & Nguyen, H. T. H. (2021). Business model innovation through the application of the Internet-of-Things: A comparative analysis. *Journal of Business Research*, 126, 126–136.

Hameed, W. U., Nisar, Q. A., & Wu, H. C. (2021). Relationships between external knowledge, internal innovation, firms' open innovation performance, service innovation and business performance in the Pakistani hotel industry. *International Journal of Hospitality Management*, 92, 102745.

Hausschildt, J., & Salomo, S. (2011). *Innovations management*. München: Wydawnictwo Vahlen, 16.

Holm, A. B., Günzel, F., & Ulhøi, J. P. (2013). Openness in innovation and business models: Lessons from the newspaper industry. *International Journal of Technology Management*, 61(3/4), 324–348.

Jabłoński, M. M. (2013). *Kształtowanie modeli biznesu w procesie kreacji wartości przedsiębiorstw* (Vol. 10). Warszawa: Difin.

Janasz, W., & Kozioł, K. (2007). *Determinanty działalności innowacyjnej przedsiębiorstw*. Warszawa: PWE, 11, 13, 14, 16.

Janulek, P. (2022). *Projektowanie modeli biznesu usług profesjonalnych w mediach społecznościowych*. Sopot: Centrum Myśli Strategicznych.

Jayadatta, S. (2024). A study on AI driven agricultural innovations for rural and industrial development in the Indian context. *Journal of Rural and Industrial Development*, 12(1), 01–16.

Koibichuk, V., Ostrovska, N., Kashiyeva, F., & Kwilinski, A. (2021). Innovation technology and cyber frauds risks of neobanks: gravity model analysis. *Marketing i menedžment innovacij*, (1), 253–265.

Kopaliński, W. (1985). *Słownik wyrazów obcych*. Warszawa: Wiedza Powszechna.

Koszany, D., & Jakubowiec, M. (2022). Transformacja cyfrowa przedsiębiorstw. *Zeszyt Naukowy, Wyższa Szkoła Zarządzania i Bankowości w Krakowie*, 66, 12–21.

Kotler, P. (1999). *Marketing Analiza, planowanie, wdrażanie i kontrola*. Warszawa: Wydawnictwo Felberg SJA, 52–55.

Kreiterling, C. (2023). Digital innovation and entrepreneurship: A review of challenges in competitive markets. *Journal of Innovation and Entrepreneurship*, 12(1), 49.

Kuczera, K. (2013). Metodyka badania modeli biznesowych podmiotów gospodarczych. *Management and Business Administration. Central Europe*, 120(1), 108–123.

Kumar, V., Alshazly, H., Idris, S. A., & Bourouis, S. (2021). Evaluating the impact of COVID-19 on society, environment, economy, and education. *Sustainability*, 13(24), 13642.

Lee, S.M., Olson, D.L., & Trimi, S. (2012). Co-innovation: Convergenomics, collaboration, and co-creation for organizational values. *Management Decision*, 5, 818–819.

Lestari, S. D., Leon, F. M., Widyastuti, S., Brabo, N. A., & Putra, A. H. P. K. (2020). Antecedents and consequences of innovation and business strategy on performance and competitive advantage of SMEs. *The Journal of Asian Finance, Economics and Business*, 7(6), 365–378.

Li, L., Msaad, H., Sun, H., Tan, M. X., Lu, Y., & Lau, A. K. (2020). Green innovation and business sustainability: New evidence from energy intensive industry in China. *International Journal of Environmental Research and Public Health*, 17(21), 7826.

Litfin, T. (2000). Adoptionsfaktoren. Empirische Analyse am Beispiel eines innovativen Telekommunikationsdienstes. Dissertationsschrift, Universitätsbibliothek Kiel, 19–20.

Machado, T. O., Stubbs, C. J., Chiaradia, V., Alraddadi, M. A., Brandolese, A., Worch, J. C., & Dove, A. P. (2024). A renewably sourced, circular photopolymer resin for additive manufacturing. *Nature*, 629(8014), 1069–1074.

Mendling, J., & Brocke, J. V. (2018). *Business process management cases: Digital innovation and business transformation in practice*. New York: Springer International Publishing AG.

Myers, S., & Marquis, D. G. (1969). *Successful industrial innovations: A study of factors underlying innovation in selected firms* (Vol. 69, No. 17). National Science Foundation.

Ngo, L. V., & O'Cass, A. (2013). Innovation and business success: The mediating role of customer participation. *Journal of Business Research*, 66(8), 1134–1142.

Ober, J. (2022). *Adaptacja innowacji w świetle zachowań organizacyjnych-wybrane aspekty*. Wydawnictwo Politechniki Śląskiej.

Olavarrieta, S., & Villena, M. G. (2014). Innovation and business research in Latin America: An overview. *Journal of Business Research*, 67(4), 489–497.

Olifirov, A. V., Makoveichuk, K. A., & Petrenko, S. A. (2019). Transformation of business models in the digital economy. *International Journal of Open Information Technologies*, 7(4), 85–91.

Ostrovska, H., Tsikh, H., Strutynska, I., Kinash, I., Pietukhova, O., Golovnya, O., & Shehynska, N. (2021). Building an effective model of intelligent entrepreneurship development in digital economy. *Eastern-European Journal of Enterprise Technologies*, 6(13), 114.

Oslo Manual. (2008). *Principles for collecting and interpreting innovation data*. Warsaw: OECD, Polish edition Ministry of Science and Higher Education.

Pomykalski A. (2001). *Zarządzanie innowacjami*. Warszara: Wydawnictwo PWN.

Prasanth, A., Densy, J. V., Surendran, P., & Bindhya, T. (2023). Role of artificial intelligence and business decision making. *International Journal of Advanced Computer Science and Applications*, 14(6).

Reformat, B. (2017). *Innowacje marketingowe w sieciach handlowych – rodzaje, obszary.* Studia Ekonomiczne. Zeszyty Naukowe Uniwersytetu Ekonomicznego w Katowicach, 321.
Rogers, E. (2003). *Diffusion of innovations.* New York: Simon and Schuster, 11.
Rohn, D., Bican, P. M., Brem, A., Kraus, S., & Clauss, T. (2021). Digital platform-based business models–An exploration of critical success factors. *Journal of Engineering and Technology Management*, 60, 101625.
Rojek, D. (2014). *Otwarte innowacje jako model interaktywnego zarządzania innowacjami.* Zeszyty Naukowe Uniwersytetu Przyrodniczo-Humanistycznego w Siedlcach Nr 101 Seria. Siedlce: Administracja i Zarządzanie, 209.
Ruiz-Real, J. L., Uribe-Toril, J., Arriaza Torres, J. A., & de Pablo Valenciano, J. (2021). Artificial intelligence in business and economics research: Trends and future. *Business Economics and Management (JBEM)*, 22(1), 98–117.
Salehi, M., & Sadeq Alanbari, S. A. (2024). Knowledge sharing barriers and knowledge sharing facilitators in innovation. *European Journal of Innovation Management*, 27(8), 2701–2721.
Schumpeter, J.A. (1912). *Theorie der wirtschaftlichen Entwicklung.* Leipzig.
Schippers, M. C., West, M. A., & Dawson, J. F. (2015). Team reflexivity and innovation: The moderating role of team context. *Journal of Management*, 41(3), 769–788.
Scuotto, A., Cicellin, M., & Consiglio, S. (2023). Social bricolage and business model innovation: a framework for social entrepreneurship organizations. *Journal of Small Business and Enterprise Development*, 30(2), 234–267.
Shree, D., Singh, R. K., Paul, J., Hao, A., & Xu, S. (2021). Digital platforms for business-to-business markets: A systematic review and future research agenda. *Journal of Business Research*, 137, 354–365.
Sobińska, M. (2014). Innowacyjne modele biznesu dla IT–wyzwania i perspektywy rozwoju. *Informatyka ekonomiczna*, 31, 126–137.
Sobińska, M. (2016). Rola IT we współczesnych modelach biznesu. *Informatyka Ekonomiczna*, 41(3), 92–105.
Stornelli, A., Ozcan, S., & Simms, C. (2021). Advanced manufacturing technology adoption and innovation: A systematic literature

review on barriers, enablers, and innovation types. *Research Policy*, 50(6), 104229.

Szpringer, W. (2008). *Wpływ wirtualizacji przedsiębiorstw na modele e-biznesu*. Warszawa: Ujęcie instytucjonalne, Oficyna Wydawnicza SGH.

Szpringer, W. (2012). *Innowacyjne modele e-biznesu*. Difin, Warszawa: Aspekty Instytucjonalne.

Szuszkiewicz, A., Twardzik, M., & Lubowiecki-Vikuk, A. (2024). Doświadczenie klienta i użytkownika elementem innowacyjnych modeli biznesowych–perspektywa startupów. *Studia i Prace Kolegium Zarządzania i Finansów*, 196, 107–122.

Vijai, C., & Wisetsri, W. (2021). Rise of artificial intelligence in healthcare startups in India. *Advances in Management*, 14(1), 48–52.

Visnjic, I., Wiengarten, F., & Neely, A. (2016). Only the brave: Product innovation, service business model innovation, and their impact on performance. *Journal of Product Innovation Management*, 33(1), 36–52.

Wielgos, D. M., Homburg, C., & Kuehnl, C. (2021). Digital business capability: its impact on firm and customer performance. *Journal of the Academy of Marketing Science*, 49(4), 762–789.

Wiśniewski, A. K. (2017). Konstrukcja modeli biznesu. *Acta Universitatis Nicolai Copernici. Zarządzanie*, 44(2), 75–85.

Wodnicka, M. (2021). Wpływ czwartej rewolucji przemysłowej na innowacyjność usług. *Optimum. Economic Studies*, 105(3), 48–59.

Yopan, M., Kasali, R., Balqiah, T. E., & Pasaribu, M. (2022). The role of digital leadership, customer orientation and business model innovation for IoT companies. *International Journal of Business*, 27(2), 1–22.

Zajda, J., & Vissing, Y. (2024). Globalisation, cultural diversity, and human rights. In *Globalisation, Cultural Diversity and Human Rights* (pp. 1–10). Cham: Springer Nature Switzerland.

Żukowska J., & Pindelski M. (2010). Rola innowacji w zarząd zaniu organizacjami – studium przypadku. *Nowoczesność przemysłu i usług - Współczesne wyzwania i uwarunkowania rozwoju przemysłu i usług*, Pyka J., (ed.). Katowice: Wydawnictwo TNOIK.

# Chapter 2

# Sustainable Innovation in Digital Environment: Determinants and Conditions of Development

## 2.1 Introduction

Innovations inspired by the concept of sustainable development have become increasingly common in recent years, yet it is still not fully understood how they are perceived within the organizations adopting them. The need for cognitive value in this area grows stronger, considering recent reviews of published research, which support the hypothesis that an increased focus on sustainability also enhances business competitiveness (Hermundsdottir & Aspelund 2021) and that it becomes a driving force associated with higher profitability and improved business performance (Cherrafi et al. 2018).

Sustainability-based innovation is a broad concept of innovation that reduces negative impacts on the ecosystem

DOI: 10.1201/9781003739364-2

and society while still delivering economic outcomes. Companies are increasingly facing challenges arising from external pressures to become more sustainable, while simultaneously struggling with high competition driven by technological advancements. From a positive perspective, such pressures ultimately generate internal motivation for companies to implement innovations aimed at improving performance in a sustainable way. From a revisionist viewpoint, sustainable innovations can lead to improved company performance in terms of increased competitive advantage, which in turn drives results in a sustainable direction.

Decision-makers need insights on how to develop effective innovation policies to achieve sustainability goals; practitioners seek knowledge about the potential financial impacts of adopting sustainability and innovation strategies; and researchers aim to understand business behavior and the ability of enterprises to generate financial value while adhering to sustainability principles.

The contribution of this chapter aims to accelerate the conceptualization of sustainable innovation by establishing a typology of narratives that is unique to the context of this type of innovation. In particular, the considerations presented offer an informal assessment of the potential to help innovators identify the most appropriate pathways for implementing sustainable innovations within their organizations.

## 2.2 Innovations through the Lens of Sustainable Development

Following Schumpeter (Schumpeter 1934), we define "innovation" as the creation of new combinations of production resources, taking into account factors of production. Schumpeter distinguishes five types of innovation: The creation of a new kind or category/quality of product, the application of a new method of production (process innovation), entry into a new market, the search for a new source of raw materials, or the establishment of a new type of business organization. Therefore, innovation is seen not only as a disruptive force but also as a learning process. Companies can either invest in the discovery of new knowledge or in the exploitation of existing knowledge. In this context, innovative organizations are viewed as agents of change who perform an entrepreneurial function. March (1991) describes the trade-off between exploration and exploitation, where "exploration includes things captured by terms such as search, variation, risk taking, experimentation, flexibility, discovery, and innovation."

The theoretical concept of innovation is expanding along with the growing complexity of the socio-economic environment. Consequently, innovation is no longer understood simply in technical terms but rather integrates innovations in products, quality, strategy, management, processes, and technology, embedding the values defined by the concept of sustainable development into the enterprise system from the stage of concept development, research and development, to commercialization.

The concept of sustainable development is defined in various ways. From the triple bottom line perspective, sustainable development refers to the integration of economic, social, and environmental pillars guiding the actions of different stakeholders (Dey et al. 2020). This issue now occupies a prominent position at the center of economic and political debate, especially after the launch of the "2030 Agenda for Sustainable Development" by the United Nations in 2015 (OECD 2017). In order to achieve the UN's 17 Sustainable Development Goals (alongside the targets established by the 2015 Paris Agreement on climate change), Sachs and others (2019) identified six major socio-economic transformations across fields such as education, health, energy and transport, and natural resources. Most of these socio-economic transitions involve the introduction and adoption of new technologies, including those related to carbon reduction, material recycling, and the improvement of human health and well-being.

Indeed, on the one hand, enhanced outcomes in the area of sustainable action cannot be achieved without innovation, while on the other, the concept of sustainable development should entail the interdependence of the social, economic, and environmental dimensions of sustainability.

These relatively easy-to-visualize assumptions at the global, national, or societal level become much more difficult to measure and implement at the level of an individual enterprise. And although sustainability was initially regarded as an added cost for businesses, recent evidence has shown that sustainable practices can create value for organizations (Van Holt et al. 2020). In fact, Kiron and others (2013) argue that most managers recognize the benefits of sustainable practices, which support shifts in priorities and operational activities across various companies. The principles of being "sustainable," "green," or "eco-friendly" reflect a resource-oriented view and assume rational corporate behavior in utilizing those resources. According to this principle, emerging products and services can be defined as those that either conserve resources or reduce pollution or waste (US Department of Commerce 2010).

A novel model of sustainable innovation that goes beyond eco-efficiency must take into account factors beyond just the characteristics of a product. Therefore, it is necessary to adopt a multi-life-cycle perspective: Natural resources can also be preserved by extending the product life cycle. Companies planning to implement the principle of sustainable innovation must change their logic of utility and rethink the purpose of the product. They could benefit from sustainability gains in the form of new business opportunities or enhanced product quality. Sustainable innovation, after all, means deriving the maximum possible utility from natural resources once they are introduced into the industrial system, regardless of whether they are part of a product, a component, or simply embedded as materials (Krikke 2011).

At the organizational level, sustainability can be broadly translated into strategies that lead to the achievement of short-term financial, social, and environmental results without compromising long-term outcomes in these areas. This means that a company must create value for its stakeholders in the present while simultaneously investing in strategies and resources to improve the social, environmental, and economic performance desired by its stakeholders (including shareholders) in the future. In doing so, the company must manage the uncertainty related to the evolving and dynamic definition of "value" among different stakeholders over time.

Sustainable actions should account for social, environmental, and economic benefits in order to achieve the goals set by customers and stakeholders (Aktin & Gergin 2016) through joint efforts (Rodriguez-Espindola et al. 2020). It is necessary to assess the potential impact of sustainable initiatives on businesses to understand the potential benefits across these dimensions. While challenges remain in incorporating social and environmental dimensions into the traditional financial performance objective, recent years have seen a growing number of publications on sustainable performance, often receiving a positive reception. The goal is to support companies in achieving economically efficient business models that can thrive despite increasingly scarce resources and overcome social challenges (Geradts & Bocken 2019).

To achieve the United Nations Sustainable Development Goals, modern enterprises must introduce a range of sustainability innovations aimed at reducing their environmental and social footprints. Innovations embedded in the concept of sustainable development can thus be defined as innovations that improve sustainability outcomes, where such outcomes encompass ecological, economic, and social criteria (Boons et al. 2013). In this way, sustainable innovations can offer a solution to the conflict between environmental and social degradation and economic development (Lin et al. 2019).

This definition of sustainability-based innovation includes a distinction between environmental and social innovations. Due to the current focus on environmental issues and climate change, environmental innovations have received more attention in recent years (Seuring & Mueller 2008) and primarily concern improvements in energy efficiency, emissions reduction, waste management, recycling, reuse, and product durability (Amores-Salvado et al. 2014). Interestingly, although environmental sustainability has attracted the most attention, it is directly related to only 6 of the 17 Sustainable Development Goals. Most of the SDGs address social challenges, yet these have received comparatively less focus in business-oriented sustainability literature (Tabares 2020).

Social sustainability is perceived differently across various disciplines. We define social innovations as those that contribute to improving quality of life, delivering social benefits, and promoting the overall public good (Dawson & Daniel 2010).

In this context, over the past decades, companies have increasingly incorporated social and environmental issues into their innovation activities, as evidenced by the growing attention to the idea of Corporate Social Responsibility (CSR), with a particular emphasis on sustainable innovation.

## 2.3 Building a Sustainable Organization

Building a sustainable organization requires a company to analyze and fundamentally revise its strategy to ensure both short-term and long-term economic, social, and environmental performance in line with the expectations of various stakeholders, including investors and shareholders. An effective strategy for generating and implementing successful sustainable innovations requires that the company (Sharma 2017):

- Identifies material and relevant sustainability issues.
- Understands the link between sustainable practices and competitive advantage.
- Builds a business logic for a sustainability strategy.
- Builds managerial motivation.
- Develops critical capabilities.

Identifying material sustainability issues requires generating data on the company's impact on sustainability, which must be addressed through a strategic analysis of the company's sustainability footprint. This includes measuring and benchmarking the company's social and environmental footprint, in addition to economic indicators, based on the materiality of issues that matter to stakeholders and assessing the impact of these issues on current and future business operations. Before developing a strategy, managers must understand both the risks associated with pursuing an unsustainable strategy and the connection between sustainable strategy and competitive advantage.

Building a business logic for a sustainable strategy requires understanding how sustainable value creates corporate value in terms of improving the core offering for the customers the company serves. Creating managerial motivation requires a mindset shift and the creation of a framework to capture opportunities and motivate employees to become agents of change within the sustainable organization. Developing critical capabilities involves embedding unique processes within the firm to engage and integrate stakeholders, generate insights and higher-order learning, and produce continuous innovation in processes, products, services, and business models that enhance sustainability performance and enable the company to compete in future markets and co-create sustainable business models.

Sustainability is rooted in profitable strategies of maintaining and revalorizing resources and products within the industrial sphere. Firstly, companies can reuse components. Secondly, life cycles can overlap when multiple, sequential use cases can be applied to the same product. For practitioners, policymakers, and researchers, it is essential to understand how adopting sustainability and innovation strategies affects overall business performance.

A sustainable organization is one that transforms its operations or strategy not only to achieve its economic or core goals (e.g., for a non-profit, this may involve providing healthcare or clean water rather than generating profits) but also to achieve its social and environmental outcomes. As such, a sustainable organization is fundamentally different from a company that does not change its core business model or strategy but simply acts responsibly by adopting practices aimed at mitigating the negative social and environmental impacts of its existing operations.

For a long time, sustainable development was separated from companies' core business strategies (Schrettle et al. 2014). In recent years, however, significant changes have occurred, and today most companies view sustainability strategies as important (Engert & Baumgartner 2016) and integrated into their core business strategy (Burki et al. 2018; Ghassim & Bogers 2019). The term *sustainability strategies* refers to "the formalization of sustainability within firms through the implementation of new planning, evaluation, and reporting procedures, in addition to new goals and responsibilities" (Reyes-Rodrigeuz et al. 2016). Moreover, the adoption of sustainability strategies signals proactive strategic behavior that is, acting in compliance with regulatory standards while actively striving to improve environmental and social performance through modifications to products, processes, and technologies that reduce negative impacts (Fraj et al. 2015; Wijethilake et al. 2018).

As a result, strategic management involves both the formulation and implementation of strategy, much like the distinction between strategic intent and actual behavior. Therefore, if there is potential for gaining a competitive advantage through sustainability, the mere creation of a sustainability strategy is not sufficient. Achieving success requires the mobilization of resources, capabilities, managerial attention, and opportunity recognition (Long et al. 2017).

Because of this, two opposing perspectives have emerged in the approach to sustainability innovation: The *traditionalist* and the *revisionist* views, contributing to heterogeneity in the current literature. The traditionalist view holds that sustainability innovations do not generate benefits for firms but only for the environment. Furthermore, sustainability innovations are seen as requiring high initial investments, offering long payback periods, and leading to increased costs, higher prices, and reduced competitiveness (Kuzma et al. 2020). The revisionist view contradicts this and suggests that sustainability innovations increase competitiveness in multiple ways that enhance various dimensions of firm performance (Ikram et al. 2020).

There are at least two reasons why sustainability strategies may not be accompanied by actual implementation. One is often referred to as *ceremonial adoption*, meaning the strategy is performed only symbolically, not in practice. This is a well-known phenomenon in the production systems literature and, in the context of sustainability, is commonly labeled *greenwashing*, where firms misrepresent their sustainability actions without genuinely implementing them (Vries et al. 2015).

Second, non-execution may also stem from implementation complexity. Implementing sustainability strategies can be difficult and time-consuming if an organization is deeply rooted in unsustainable practices and if implementation requires significant changes in structure, practices, mindset, and resource commitment (Engert & Baumgartner 2016). On this basis, it can be assumed that there is potential to improve firm performance by increasing value creation or reducing business costs or risks. However, firms that adopt sustainability strategies only ceremonially or fail to implement them for other reasons are unable to realize these benefits.

Ultimately, strategy is about managing how resources and capabilities are deployed in actual behavior (Bacinello et al. 2019).

Given that innovation has long been recognized as a key driver of sustainable development, its creation and advancement are increasingly becoming an integral part of a company's vision and overall strategy for long-term success. However, the multiple interpretations of sustainability within organizations can have significant consequences for the outcomes of sustainability initiatives.

In many organizational cultures, sustainability narratives are used as tools for meaning-making among individuals and over time, and the very understanding of the concept of corporate sustainability may have unintended positive and negative consequences for the implementation of corporate social responsibility.

## 2.4 Framework and Drivers of Sustainable Innovation

Sustainable innovation, also known as green innovation, environmental innovation, or ecological innovation, refers to the ability of enterprises to reduce their environmental impact or achieve specific ecological sustainability goals by introducing new ideas, behaviors, products, and processes. These include new eco-friendly products, new environmental protection technologies, and the integration of ecological and sustainable development principles in the exploitation and redevelopment of new markets, new processes, and new systems (Blattel-Mink 1998), thus aligning with the trend of improving environmental conditions and achieving environmental benefits (Mirata & Emtairah 2005).

The concept of sustainable innovation, in the context of identified societal challenges, is not limited solely to the environment and climate change but encompasses a broad range of social issues. Among these, particular attention should be paid to employee health and safety. Therefore, it can be argued that enterprises (and their production processes) cannot be defined as "sustainable" without ensuring the safety and well-being of their most essential resource.

Sustainable innovations can be seen as a direction that promotes competitiveness, human and social well-being, and environmentally friendly practices (Adams et al. 2016; Khurana et al. 2021; Klewitz & Hansen 2014). Adams and others (2016) identify innovation practices that support sustainability at the product, process, and organizational levels. Product innovations involve introducing improvements or entirely new products or services to enhance sustainable performance (Klewitz & Hansen 2014). While sustainable innovation is a rapidly evolving field, it has primarily focused on product innovation but is now increasingly encompassing process and organizational changes as well.

At the process level, sustainable innovations encourage organizations to redesign their operations to reduce resource consumption, improve the management of non-product elements, and introduce eco-efficiency into their activities. At the organizational level, such innovations require the implementation of strategic behaviors aligned with sustainability principles. This includes cultural change supported by life cycle thinking, the implementation of integrated sustainability strategies, and the introduction of environmental management systems. The motivation lies in consolidating organizational practices and values in relation to processes, products, and human resources in order to achieve environmental and social goals, ultimately leading to economic productivity (Abdul-Rashid Salwa et al. 2017).

A straightforward understanding of the concept of sustainable innovation involves two key terms: Sustainable development and innovation. However, many researchers challenge this seemingly obvious interpretation, arguing that sustainable development should not be reduced solely to ecology and the green environment, nor innovation to merely technological aspects. Such a narrow view would imply that sustainable innovation is limited to technological modernization in the environmental and ecological domains.

Jorna (2017) offers an alternative interpretation, suggesting that environmental sustainability is always directly or indirectly tied to how people possess and organize knowledge. The management and operationalization of this knowledge occur within organizations, corporations, enterprises, and institutions. In this view, innovation may involve abandoning something existing and replacing it with something new. Just like products, services, and organizations themselves can be innovative, good innovation always results in the creation of knowledge in a specific context.

Sustainable innovation is also described in the literature as "making intentional changes in an organization's philosophy and values, as well as its products, processes, and practices, to serve a specific purpose of creating and realizing social and environmental value alongside economic profit" (Adams et al. 2016). Across organizations, definitions, cultures, criteria, and expectations guiding sustainable innovations vary greatly, as evidenced in numerous typologies and classifications.

Sustainable innovation refers to transforming existing products and processes into more sustainable versions (Albort-Morant et al. 2016). Its goal is to create or improve products and processes in order to keep resource use and waste generation within acceptable environmental limits (Foxon & Pearson 2008). This includes innovations in product and process technologies that are essential for energy saving, pollution prevention, waste recycling, eco-design, or corporate environmental management (Chen et al. 2006). Emissions reduction, recycling, and minimizing material and resource consumption are key aspects of sustainable process innovation. Choosing less polluting materials, using fewer resources, and designing products that are easier to recycle, reuse, or biodegrade are core to sustainable product innovation.

Sustainable innovations are achieved through knowledge creation, and the methods and structures embedding this knowledge in organizations should be actively supported. A proper innovation process ensures that knowledge becomes sustainable. The essence of sustainable innovation is shaped by a process-oriented view of sustainable development. Whenever we refer to a product, production process, or service as sustainable, we mean that a balance has been achieved between the three pillars of sustainability—*Planet*, *profit*, and *people*, with *planet* often being the most emphasized. A car may be considered sustainable because it runs on hydrogen, or electricity may be seen as sustainable because it's generated from biomass. In the same way, we say that an innovation can be sustainable, for example, a new material is discovered that is less harmful to the environment, or a new production process is developed that generates fewer harmful emissions. These are clear examples of sustainable innovation (Jorna 2017).

In general, innovation requires companies to actively build, adapt, and apply knowledge across functional boundaries to solve problems (Leonard-Barton 1995). These demands also apply to sustainable innovations, which require firms to integrate environmental ideas into their innovation processes. It can thus be assumed that companies achieve better results in sustainable innovation through organizational learning. If knowledge created in one part of a company can be effectively used elsewhere, innovation improves (Knott 2003). Organizational learning is, therefore, considered directly linked to a firm's capacity for innovation, as it enables the recognition, assimilation, and application of new information (Brown & Duguid 1991; Cohen & Levinthal 1990).

Existing research indicates that learning drives innovation, and that sustainable products and process innovations are fueled by dynamic internal processes within firms (Albort-Morant et al. 2016).

When analyzing the concept of sustainable innovation, it is important to note that both academic debate and empirical research on companies engaged in sustainability practices are heavily focused on so-called *eco-innovations* (Chindime et al. 2017). Indeed, due to growing concerns about global warming, environmental pollution, and the increasing scarcity of energy and resources, such innovations have become central to environmental policy and corporate innovation strategies.

Environmental innovations mainly involve new or improved products (goods or services) and processes that benefit the environment by reducing or preventing environmental harm (Rennings 2000). The concept of eco-innovation is associated with entities that develop, apply, or introduce new ideas, behaviors, products, and processes that contribute to reducing environmental burdens or achieving environmentally defined sustainability goals. These innovations aim to conserve natural resources during production, consumption, and end-of-life phases of products. Over time, companies gradually but not abruptly enhance the environmental friendliness of successive product generations.

However, innovative practices tend to favor incremental improvements, while often overlooking more radical approaches to innovation. Moreover, in recent decades, companies have also been increasingly expected to take responsibility for other social issues, including employee health and safety in the face of illnesses, accidents, and hazards (ILO 2024). To address these challenges, companies may introduce or implement health and safety innovations, which involve new technologies designed to provide workers with the best possible protection and specialized equipment, as well as new techniques, procedures, and tools that make tasks less burdensome and easier to perform.

A novel model of sustainable innovation that goes beyond eco-efficiency must consider aspects beyond just product features. According to Slowak and Regenfelder (2017), it is necessary to adopt a multi-life-cycle perspective: Natural resources can also be conserved by extending and prolonging product life. Companies implementing this new principle of sustainable innovation must, therefore, change their utility logic and rethink the purpose of the product. They would, however, benefit from sustainability-related advantages in the form of new business opportunities or improved product quality. In this approach, sustainable innovation means deriving the greatest possible utility from natural resources once they are introduced into the industrial system, regardless of whether they are embodied in a product, component, or embedded as raw materials (Krikke 2011).

Compared to other types of innovation, sustainable innovations are likely to be more complex, characterized by a higher degree of novelty, diversity, and risk (De Marchi 2012). In this area, inexperienced firms face multiple sources of uncertainty, as there are no universally accepted standards in terms of technology, production processes, or environmental performance metrics. As Horbach and others (2012) emphasize, environmental innovations rely on a broad knowledge base. Consequently, not only internal R&D activities (especially those focused on environmental issues) but, more importantly, interaction with multiple sources of external knowledge is likely to be more crucial for sustainable innovation than for other types of innovation. This can be explained by the fact that, apart from eco-industries whose core activity is developing green technologies, most firms require knowledge and skills for eco-innovation that fall outside their core competencies (Gonzalez-Moreno et al. 2019).

First and foremost, within an organization, innovation can be directed toward sustainable services, products, or production processes. Take, for example, hydrogen technology, which is increasingly seen as a key technology for the near future, provided hydrogen is not produced by burning natural gas, oil, or coal. Hydrogen as an energy source is efficient, can be used on a small scale, and has high output. It also avoids the environmental downsides associated with biomass and fossil fuels, the cost issues of solar panels, and the low efficiency of wind energy. Consider a company that, through innovation, develops an effective method for transitioning from gas and oil as energy carriers to hydrogen technology as an energy supplier. This company would be engaging in sustainable innovation.

Secondly, sustainable innovation can also refer to organizing innovation itself in a sustainable way. This means that the innovation process is constructed as an integral part of the organization's value chain. As a result, sustainable innovation reaches into the core of a business or organization, especially into its knowledge processes. The goal of this approach is to influence how people within the organization deal with knowledge how it is acquired and collected, how it is shared, and how it is applied. In essence, sustainable innovation concerns knowledge-based processes at the heart of the organization. It influences the way the organization manages knowledge. The innovation process is inherently linked to all forms of knowledge creation and management. It is very difficult for organizations as complex systems or innovations and transitions as complex situations to define a fixed state of sustainability. Enterprises or innovations cannot be assessed based on a fixed degree of sustainability, because sustainability is a dynamic process, and both innovations and businesses constantly evolve.

However, there is more to it. For complex systems like firms, enterprises, and organizations, or complex processes like innovations, it is very difficult to define a "sustainable state." The sustainability level of a company or innovation cannot simply be measured, because it changes over time. Therefore, we suggest replacing the term "sustainable development" with "sustaining." By "sustaining," we aim to highlight the fact that organizational processes are in continuous flux. The same applies to innovation. Innovation does not exist for a fixed period and then ends; it continues as a process rather than a project. Still, the innovation process must constantly focus on sustainability. Consequently, from the perspective of the humanities and organizational sciences, design principles must be formulated and implemented in such a way that the innovation process remains sustainable over time.

Thus, reevaluating goods, products, and materials becomes central to new patterns of sustainable innovation. Companies can "save" resources by using fewer materials during production, designing products that are resource-efficient during use, or facilitating reuse after the first usage phase. They can also recover resources from discarded products. This approach challenges the old innovation model, where innovation was often measured primarily by the number of new products introduced. The proposed principle of sustainable innovation conserves resources, is inclusive, and life-cycle oriented. The novel pattern includes new ways of linking product development with the revaluation and reuse of products. Manufacturers and suppliers extend the life of a new product by placing it in a new usage context or recovering components and raw materials. At the end of various life phases, such as in primary and secondary industrial use, valuable raw materials are recovered. The life cycles of product materials and even of markets begin to overlap, and the value chain becomes fully enclosed in a circular loop.

## 2.5 Key Factors Influencing the Development of Sustainable Innovations

The previously presented conceptualization of sustainable innovation clearly emphasized its interdisciplinary nature. Karakaya and others (2014) argue that sustainable innovation spans three interdisciplinary fields: Economics, sociology, and management, as well as marketing. From an economic perspective, the key focus is to examine the drivers of innovation, strategies, and mechanisms behind sustainable innovative behavior in firms, while continuously addressing two questions: Can sustainable innovation be considered a "normal innovation," and does it require its own theory for explanation and investigation (Rennings 2000)?

Many perspectives maintain that traditional economic theory is useful and effective in analyzing sustainable innovative behavior in enterprises. However, others highlight that, compared to general innovation, sustainable innovation beyond the typical spillover effect *(the knowledge spillover effect occurs when innovations or technologies developed by an organization through R&D activities become freely and publicly accessible to other enterprises that were in no way involved in their creation)* (Augustyn 2017) also generates an externality by reducing production-related or environmental external costs of products, referred to as a "double externality effect" (Rennings 2000).

Therefore, it is necessary to identify the determinants of sustainable innovation development and to assess whether conventional factors can drive sustainable innovation. This subsection analyses the determinants of corporate sustainable innovativeness from a multidimensional perspective, including:

- Supply-side factors (technological capabilities and market characteristics),
- Demand-side factors (expected market demand and public awareness regarding environmental protection), and
- Regulatory and policy influences (environmental policies and regulatory frameworks) (Wei et al. 2022).

Factors facilitating the adoption of sustainable innovations have been identified largely as external pressures and internal motivation (Díaz-García et al. 2015).

Sustainable innovation behavior in companies is shaped by internal factors such as corporate governance, financial performance, environmental strategy, and management team characteristics, as well as by external pressures including regulatory support, intellectual property protection, and market networks.

The identification of internal factors influencing the innovative behavior of traditional firms is largely based on the resource-based view (RBV), which emphasizes the role of firm heterogeneity and internal attributes in overall innovativeness (Vega-Jurado et al. 2008). From this perspective, sustainable innovative behavior can also be interpreted through the resource-based lens, recognizing that each company possesses a unique set of resources and capabilities, which in turn determine whether it notices, pursues, and participates in strategic decisions related to sustainable innovation. According to the RBV theory, several internal factors can be identified as influential in sustainable innovativeness.

First, sustainable innovation requires adequate resource support (e.g., capital, labor, materials, and technology). Therefore, the better a company's financial performance, the more likely it is to fund and sustain long-term sustainable innovation (Li et al. 2017). Second, a sound corporate governance system is key to a company's engagement in sustainable innovation, as it reflects the company's capacity to improve efficiency, reduce risks, and maintain sustainable growth. Third, there is a strong link between sustainable innovation and its strategic implementation, particularly in terms of environmental management and environmental contributions. In general, effective environmental management can stimulate sustainable innovation, meaning that promoting environmental governance in companies can enhance green investment and improve sustainable innovation capabilities (Inoue et al. 2013). Additionally, factors such as corporate investment in environmental management and knowledge sharing (Wong 2013) have been found to positively impact a company's level of sustainable innovation.

In the context of knowledge sharing, the development of sustainable innovation at the firm level also depends on a company's interaction with external knowledge and information sources, as well as the adoption of specific human resource management (HRM) practices. Interaction with external actors and stakeholders is widely recognized as a key feature of sustainable innovation (Silvestre & Tirca 2019) and has been extensively studied in the eco-innovation literature (Gonzalez-Moreno et al. 2019; Marzucchi & Montresor 2017). However, there is still a limited understanding of how various external knowledge sources, information, and even pressures may affect other dimensions of sustainable innovation, such as improvements in occupational health and safety.

Another relatively underexplored issue is the potential role of HRM practices in guiding responsible corporate behavior (Wright et al. 2003). In general, HRM has been recognized as a fundamental tool for improving a company's innovation outcomes by empowering employees.

An additional internal factor is the characteristics of managers, which influence their strategic choices and those choices, in turn, shape the firm's innovative behavior. While innovation plays a key role in a company's survival, making an organization innovative is not simple. By identifying contextual factors, managers can help decide how to deploy a portfolio of innovation management processes. This upper echelons theory also applies to corporate sustainable innovation (Hambrick & Mason 1984). Different traits of corporate executives lead to variation in environmental management strategies, thereby affecting a firm's sustainable innovation performance.

Recent research suggests that sustainability-oriented innovation may require different organizational conditions than those identified in traditional innovation studies. More specifically, nature-inspired innovations have become increasingly common in recent years, yet it is still not fully understood how they are perceived in the organizations adopting them. A manager's interpretation of environmental issues as either opportunities or threats significantly affects the firm's strategic innovation choices. In particular, if managers prioritize environmental and social issues, firms are more likely to adopt sustainable practices (Meada et al. 2022). Specific characteristics of top management, such as tenure, education level, age, productivity, and background in R&D and technology, play a significant role in shaping sustainable innovation.

A major finding in classical innovation economics is that firm innovativeness is heavily dependent on external resources (Fagerberg & Mowery 2006). Likewise, sustainable innovation is also influenced by external factors. First, based on stakeholder theory (Murillo-Luna et al. 2008), it is emphasized that regulatory agencies and governments are key stakeholders influencing corporate behavior, and effective management of these relationships is a fundamental starting point for implementing sustainable innovation strategies.

Second, according to new institutional theory, pressure from mandatory government regulations and competition can effectively encourage firms to adopt sustainable innovation practices. These two external factors, environmental regulation and institutional pressure, are particularly important from the perspective of top management. Regulatory requirements and institutional expectations prompt firms to strengthen their environmental legitimacy, enabling the development and improvement of sustainable innovation (Berrone et al. 2013).

Other studies emphasize the importance of governmental support for innovation. For example, government subsidies provide funding sources, alleviate financial shortages, and reduce the costs associated with sustainable innovation (Montmartin & Herrera 2015). Furthermore, institutional infrastructure created by the state also impacts firm-level sustainable innovation. The more robust the legal and regulatory system for intellectual property protection, the more objectively and fairly relevant laws and regulations can be enforced, and the more effectively firms' innovative achievements can be protected.

The second external factor is the analysis from the perspective of market networks. In market competition, enterprises observe the behavior of organizations or competitors within their social networks. As a result, they are likely to implement sustainable innovations in order to secure resources and development opportunities within institutional frameworks. As Genchev (2009) stated, effective green innovation has become an important source of differentiation for enterprises in gaining a competitive advantage. Moreover, customer demand, as a primary normative pressure, is a major driving force behind corporate sustainable innovation. As public awareness of environmental protection grows, the preference of consumers and supply chain partners for eco-friendly products has become a core motivation for companies to adopt sustainable innovations. This helps maintain relationships not only between businesses and consumers but also between companies and their suppliers and network partners.

## References

Abdul-Rashid Salwa, H., Sakundarini, N., Raja Ghazilla Raja, A., & Thurasamy, R. (2017). The impact of sustainable manufacturing practices on sustainability performance: Empirical evidence from Malaysia. *International Journal of Operations and Production Management*, 37, 182–204.

Adams, R., Jeanrenaud, S., Bessant, J., Denyer, D., & Overy, P. (2016). Sustainability-oriented innovation: A systematic review. *International Journal of Management Reviews*, 18(2), 180–205. https://doi.org/10.1111/ijmr.12068

Aktin, T., & Gergin, Z. (2016). Mathematical modelling of sustainable procurement strategies: Three case studies. *Journal of Cleaner Production*, 113, 767–780.

Albort-Morant, G., Leal-Millan, A., & Cepeda-Carrion, G. (2016). The antecedents of green innovation performance: A model of learning and capabilities. *Journal of Business Research*, 69(11), 4912–4917.

Amores-Salvado, J., Martin-de Castro, G., & Navas-Lopez, J. E. (2014). Green corporate image: Moderating the connection between environmental product innovation and firm performance. *Journal of Cleaner Production*, 83, 356–365.

Augustyn, A. (2017). *Efekty spillover w procesach innowacyjnych*. Wrocław: Wydawnictwo Uniwersytetu Ekonomicznego we Wrocławiu.

Bacinello, E., Tontini, G., & Alberton, A. (2019). Influence of maturity on corporate social responsibility and sustainable innovation in business performance. *Corporate Social Responsibility and Environmental Management*, 27(2), 749–759.

Berrone, P., Fosfuri, A., Gelabert, L., & Gomez-Mejia, L. R. (2013). Necessity as the mother of "green" inventions: Institutional pressures and environmental innovations. *Strategic Management Journal*, 34(8), 891–909.

Blattel-Mink, B. (1998). Innovation towards sustainable economy - The integration of economy and ecology in companies. *Sustainable Development*, 6(2), 49–58.

Boons, F., Montalvo, C., Quist, J., & Wagner, M. (2013). Sustainable innovation, business models, and economic performance: An overview. *Journal of Cleaner Production*, 45, 1–8.

Brown, J. S., & Duguid, P. (1991). Organizational learning and communities-of-practice: Toward a unified view of working, learning and innovation. *Organization Science*, 2(1), 40–57.

Burki, U., Ersoy, P., & Dahlstrom, R. (2018). Achieving triple bottom line performance in manufacturer-customer supply chains: Evidence from an emerging economy. *Journal of Cleaner Production*, 197, 1307–1316.

Chen, Y. S., Lai, S. B., & Wen, C. T. (2006). The influence of green innovation performance on corporate advantage in Taiwan. *Journal of Business Ethics*, 67(4), 331–339.

Cherrafi, A., Garza-Reyes, J. A., Kumar, V., Mishra, N., Ghobadian, A., & Elfezazi, S. (2018). Lean, green practices and process innovation: A model for green supply chain performance. *International Journal of Production Economics*, 206, 79–92. https://doi.org/10.1016/j.ijpe.2018.09.031

Chindime, S., Kibwika, P., & Chagunda, M. (2017). Determinants of sustainable innovation performance by smallholder dairy farmers in Malawi. *Cogent Food and Agriculture*, 3(1). https://doi.org/10.1080/23311932.2017.1379292

Cohen, W. M., & Levinthal, D. A. (1990). Absorptive capacity: A new perspective on learning and innovation. *Administrative Science Quarterly*, 35(1), 128–152.

Dawson, P., & Daniel, L. (2010). Understanding social innovation: A provisional framework. *International Journal Technological Management*, 51(1), 9–21.

Dey, P. K., Malesios, C., De, D., Chowdhury, S., & Abdelaziz, F. B. (2020). The impact of lean management practices and sustainability-oriented innovation on sustainability performance of small and medium-sized enterprises: Empirical evidence from the UK. *British Journal of Management*, 31(1), 141–161.

Díaz-García, C., Gonzalez-Moreno, Á., & Saez-Martinez, F. J. (2015). Eco-innovation: Insight from a literature review. *Innovation: Management Policy & Practice*, 17, 6–23.

Engert, S., & Baumgartner, R. J. (2016). Corporate sustainability strategy - Bridging the gap between formulation and implementation. *Journal of Cleaner Production*, 113, 822–834.

Fagerberg, J., & Mowery, D. C. (2006). *The Oxford handbook of innovation*. Oxford, UK: Oxford University Press.

Foxon, T., & Pearson, P. (2008). Overcoming barriers to innovation and diffusion of cleaner technologies: Some features of a sustainable innovation policy regime. *Journal of Cleaner Production*, 16(1), 148–161.

Fraj, E., Matute, J., & Melero, I. (2015). Environmental strategies and organizational competitiveness in the hotel industry: The role of learning and innovation as determinants of environmental success. *Tourism Management*, 46, 30–42.

Genchev, S. E. (2009). Revers logistics program design: A company study. *Business Horizons*, 52(2), 139–148.

Geradts, T. H. J., & Bocken, N. M. P. (2019). Driving sustainability-oriented innovation. *MIT Sloan Management Review*, 78–83.

Ghassim, B., & Bogers, M. (2019). Linking stakeholders engagement to profitability through sustainability-oriented innovation: A quantitative study of the minerals industry. *Journal of Cleaner Production*, 224AD, 905–919.

Gonzalez-Moreno, A., Trigueno, A., & Saez-Martinez, F. J. (2019). Many of trusted partners for eco-innovation? The influence of breadth and depth of firms' knowledge network in the food sector. *Technological Forecasting and Social Change*, 147, 51–62.

Hambrick, D. C., & Mason, P. A. (1984). Upper echelons: The organization as the reflection of its top managers. *Academy of Management Journal*, 9(2), 193–206.

Hermundsdottir, F., & Aspelund, A. (2021). Sustainability innovations and firm competitiveness: A review. *Journal of Cleaner Production*, 280, 124715.

Van Holt, T., Statler, M., Atz, U., Whelan, T., van Loggerenberg, M., & Cebulla, J. (2020). The cultural consensus of sustainability-driven innovation: Strategies for success. *Business Strategy and the Environment*, 29, 3399–3409.

Horbach, J., Rammer, C., & Rennings, K. (2012). Determinants of eco-innovations by type of environmental impact - The role of regulatory push/pull, technology push and market pull. *Ecological Economics*, 78, 112–122.

Ikram, M., Zhang, Q., Sroufe, R., & Ferasso, M. (2020). The social dimensions of corporate sustainability: An integrative framework including COVID-19 insights. *Sustainability*, 12.8747.

ILO. (2024). Safety and health at work: A vision for sustainable prevention. *XX World Congress on Safety and Health at Work 2014: Global Forum for Prevention*.

Inoue, E., Arimura, T. H., & Nakano, M. (2013). A new insight into environmental innovation: Does the maturity of environmental management systems matter? *Ecological Economics*, 94, 156–163.

Jorna, R., ed. (2017). *Sustainable innovation. The organisational, human and knowledge dimension*. London, UK: Routledge Taylor & Francis Group.

Karakaya, E., Hidalgo, A., & Nuur, C. (2014). Diffusion of eco-innovations: A review. *Renewable and Sustainable Energy Reviews*, 33, 392–399.

Khurana, S., Haleem, A., Luthra, S., & Mannan, B. (2021). Evaluating critical factors to implement sustainable oriented innovation practices: An analysis of micro, small, and medium manufacturing enterprises. *Journal of Cleaner Production*, 285, 125377.

Kiron, D., Kruschwitz, N., Reeves, M., & Goh, E. (2013). The benefits of sustainability-driven innovation. *MIT Sloan Management Review*, 54, 69–73.

Klewitz, J., & Hansen, E. G. (2014). Sustainability-oriented innovation of SMEs: A systematic review. *Journal of Cleaner Production*, 65(15), 57–75.

Knott, A. M. (2003). Persistent heterogeneity and sustainable innovation. *Strategic Management Journal*, 24(8), 687–705.

Krikke, H. (2011). Impact of closed-loop network configurations on carbon footprints: A case study. *Resources, Conservation and Recycling*, 55(12), 1196–1205.

Kuzma, E., Padilha, L. S., Sehnem, S., Julkovski, D. J., & Roman, D. J. (2020). The relationship between innovation and sustainability: A meta-analytic study. *Journal of Cleaner Production*, 259, 120745.

Leonard-Barton, D. (1995). *Wellsprings of knowledge: Building and sustaining the sources of innovation*. Boston, MA: Harvard Business Review School Press.

Li, D., Zheng, M., Cao, C., Chen, X., Ren, S., & Huang, M. (2017). The impact of legitimacy pressure and corporate profitability on green innovation: Evidence from China Top 100. *Journal of Cleaner Production*, 141, 41–49.

Lin, W. L., Cheah, J. H., Azali, M., Ho, J. A., & Yip, N. (2019). Does firm size matter? Evidence on the impact of the green innovation strategy on corporate financial performance in the automotive sector. *Journal of Cleaner Production*, 229, 974–988.

Long, X., Chen, Y., Du, J., Oh, K., Han, I., & Yan, J. (2017). The effect of environmental innovation behavior on economic and environmental performance of 182 Chinese firms. *Journal of Cleaner Production*, 166, 1274–1282.

March, J. G. (1991). Exploration and exploitation in organizational learning. *Organization Science*, 2(1), 71–87.

De Marchi, V. (2012). Environmental innovation and R&D cooperation: Empirical evidence from Spanish manufacturing firms. *Research Policy*, 41(3), 614–923.

Marzucchi, A., & Montresor, S. (2017). Forms of knowledge and eco-innovation modes: Evidence from Spanish manufacturing firms. *Ecological Economics*, 131, 208–221.

Meada, T., Jeanrenaudb, S., & Bessantc, J. (2022). Sustainability oriented innovation narratives: Learning from nature inspired innovation. *Journal of Cleaner Production*, 344, 130980. https://doi.org/10.1016/j.jclepro.2022.130980

Mirata, M., & Emtairah, T. (2005). Industrial symbiosis networks and the contribution to environmental innovation: The case of the Landskrona industrial symbiosis programme. *Journal of Cleaner Production*, 13(10/11), 993–1002.

Montmartin, B., & Herrera, M. (2015). Internal and external effects of R&D subsidies and fiscal incentives: Empirical evidence using spatial dynamic panel models. *Research Policy*, 44(5), 1065–1079.

Murillo-Luna, J. L., Garces-Ayerbe, C., & Rivera-Torres, P. (2008). Why do patterns of environmental response differ? A stakeholders' pressure approach'. *Strategic Management Journal*, 29(11), 1225–1240.

OECD. (2017). *Agenda Na Rzecz Zrównoważonego Rozwoju 2030: W Kierunku Pozytywnego Wdrożenia w Polsce*. Seria 'Lepsza Polityka Państwa'. OECD Publishing, Retrieved from https://www.oecd.org/content/dam/oecd/pl.publications/reports/2017/11/the-2030-sustainable-development-agenda_g1g86f10/9789264265981-pl.pdf

Rennings, K. (2000). Redefining innovation - Eco-innovation research and the contribution from ecological economics. *Ecological Economics*, 32(2), 319–332. https://doi.org/10.1016/S0921-8009(99)00112-3

Reyes-Rodrigeuz, J. F., Ulhoi, J. P., & Madsen, H. (2016). Corporate environmental sustainabilityin Danish SMEs: A longitudinal study of motivators, initiatives, and strategic effects. *Corporate Social Responsibility and Environmental Management*, 23(4), 193–212.

Rodriguez-Espindola, O., Alem, D., & Pelegrin Da Silva, L. (2020). A shortage risk mitigation model for multi-agency coordination in logistics planning. *Computer & Industrial Engineering*, 148, 106676.

Sachs, J., Schmidt-Traub, G., Mazzucato, M., & Inni, I. (2019). Six transformations to achieve the sustainable goals. *Nature Sustainability*, 2, 805–814.

Schrettle, S., Hinz, A., Scherrer-Rathje, M., & Friedli, T. (2014). Turning sustainability into action: Explaining firms' sustainability efforts and their impact on firm performance. *International Journal of Production Economics*, 147, 73–84.

Schumpeter, J. A. (1934). *The theory of economic development: An inquiry into profits, capital. credit, interest, and the business cycle*. Cambridge, MA: Harvard University Press. Reprinted 1983 by Transaction.

Seuring, S., & Mueller, M. (2008). From a literature review to a conceptual framework for sustainable supply chain management. *Journal of Cleaner Production*, 16(15), 1699–1710.

Sharma, S. (2017). *Competing for a sustainable world: Building capacity for sustainable innovation*. London, UK: Routledge, 1–216. https://doi.org/10.4324/9781351285803

Silvestre, B., & Tirca, D. (2019). Innovations for sustainable development: Moving toward a sustainable future. *Journal of Cleaner Production*, 208, 325–332.

Slowak, A. P., & Regenfelder, M. (2017). Creating value, not wasting resources: Sustainable innovation strategies. *Innovation:*

*The European Journal of Social Science Research*, 30(4), 455–475. https://doi.org/10.1080/13511610.2016.1192990

Tabares, S. (2020). Insights from corporate social innovation: A research agenda. *Social Entrepreurship*, 16(3), 317–338.

US Department of Commerce. (2010). *Measuring the green economy, report*. Washington, DC: Economics and Statistics Administration. https://www.commerce.gov/

Vega-Jurado, J., Gutierrez-Gracia, A., Fernandez-de-Lucio, I., & Manjarres-Henriquez, L. (2008). The effect of external and internal factors on firms' product innovation. *Research Policy*, 37(4), 616–632.

Vries, G., Terwel, B. W., Ellemers, N., & Daamen, D. D. (2015). Sustainability or profitability? How communicated motives for environmental policy affect public perceptions of corporate greenwashing. *Corporate Social Responsibility and Environmental Management*, 22(3), 142–154.

Wei, J., Li, Y., Liu, X., & Du, Y. (2022). Enterprise characteristics and external influencing factors of sustainable innovation: Based on China's innovation survey. *Journal of Cleaner Production*, 372, 133461. https://doi.org/10.1016/j.jclepro.2022.133461

Wijethilake, C., Munir, R., & Appuhami, R. (2018). Environmental innovation strategy and organizational performance: Enabling and controlling uses of management control systems. *Journal of Business Ethics*, 151(4), 1139–1160.

Wong, S. K. S. (2013). Environmental requirements, knowledge sharing and green innovation: Empirical evidence from the electronics industry in China. *Business Strategy and the Environment*, 22(5), 321–338.

Wright, P., Gardner, T., & Moynihan, L. (2003). The impact of HR practices on the performance of business units. *Human Resource Management Journal*, 13(3), 21–36.

# Chapter 3

# Enterprise Financial Management in the Digital Age

## 3.1 Introduction

In the digital age, where the boundaries between the virtual and real worlds are becoming increasingly fluid, cybersecurity has evolved from a niche area of focus to a key component of national, economic, and corporate security strategies. Businesses, regardless of size or industry, are on the plane of this change, facing increasingly complex and sophisticated digital threats. In a turbulent environment characterized by rapid technological, political, and societal changes, cybersecurity management requires not only reactive actions but above all a proactive attitude and adaptive strategies (Antczak 2024). The management of modern organizations is characterized by high complexity and changeability of conditions. On a daily basis, managers have to face challenges such as globalization, dynamic ICT development, cultural diversity, variability of legal and system regulations, increasing dynamics of business processes, and growing customer expectations. In these

DOI: 10.1201/9781003739364-3

conditions, the professionalization of management, consisting of the creation of system solutions and their management with the use of specific tools, becomes a necessity. An intuitive approach, variability of rules of operation, lack of vision, and low efficiency of organizational processes are the main factors of failure in modern management (Czekaj & Ziębicki 2021). Each organizational unit, in order to function properly in a competitive environment, must be properly managed. Management is a complex process that involves all links in the organization's operations. The specificity of the organization is always associated with a multifaceted management process. Management is about making the right management decisions, thanks to which the organization is able to function properly and achieve its goals (Antczak 2020).

Artificial intelligence (AI) applications, such as predictive analytics, process automation, and fraud prevention systems, enable executives around the world to increase operational efficiency and precision in enterprise decision-making. Research prepared by PwC in 2024 shows that more than 55% of companies plan to significantly increase investments in AI-based solutions in the coming years, recognizing their potential to optimize costs, shorten task completion times, and minimize errors. According to the report, the financial sector is a leader in the implementation of AI. About 50% of organizations declare having a defined strategy for the use of AI for the next 3–5 years, and 30% of the surveyed companies are working intensively on the implementation of these solutions, with a plan to be completed within 12 months (PwC 2024). On the other hand, research conducted by McKinsey & Company (2023) indicates that companies using advanced data analytics and AI report higher operational efficiency compared to those that have not implemented such technologies. Moreover, the automation of financial management processes reduces the risk of errors, which is crucial in compliance with legal regulations and increasing competitiveness.

This chapter analyses selected financial management tools that combine modern technologies and are also necessary for effective business activity. The aim of the chapter is to indicate that financial management is one of the most important levels in both current and long-term management of the company's operations, as well as to examine the potential of using AI as a tool supporting financial management in the company.

Financial management in the digital age is not only a necessity but also an opportunity for growth, innovation, and competitiveness. Companies that successfully implement modern financial technologies can gain a significant advantage in the market.

## 3.2 Corporate Finance Management in Cyberspace

Corporate financial management focuses on decisions about the value and type of assets to be acquired and conducting business in such a way as to maximize the value of those assets (Brigham & Houston 2015). Enterprise financial management includes processes related to the acquisition, allocation, and use of financial resources in order to maximize the value of the enterprise. The key areas of financial management are financial planning, cost control, working capital management, capital structure, and investment decisions (Brigham 2019; Ross et al. 2021; Van Horne & Wachowicz 2015). Financial planning includes cash flow forecasting, cost analysis, and determining the company's financing strategy. Financial analysis helps to assess the condition of the company, using, for example, profitability, liquidity, debt, and operational efficiency ratios (Fabozzi & Drake 2009; Gitman & Zutter 2019; Higgins et al. 2023). Cost control is the process of monitoring, analyzing, and managing expenses[1] to achieve specific financial goals, such as minimizing costs, increasing operational efficiency, and improving profitability. It includes identifying and eliminating unnecessary expenses, optimizing resource allocation for the best return on investment.

Effective working capital management includes the management of receivables, inventories, and short-term liabilities, which affects the financial liquidity and profitability of the company (Arnold 2019; Brealey et al. 2022; Petersen & Rajan 1997). Decisions concerning the capital structure include selecting debt financing versus own capital. Capital structure theories such as the Modigliani–Miller theory, compromise theory, and financing hierarchy theory may help in structuring a financial policy of an enterprise (Graham & Harvey 2001; Modigliani & Miller 1958; Myers 1984). Access to sources of finance, such as bank loans, the issuance of shares, and bonds, is crucial for the growth of companies. Capital market analysis helps in making decisions regarding the issuance of securities (Baker & Wurgler 2002; Demirgüç-Kunt & Maksimovic 1998; Zingales 1998). Companies use risk management strategies such as hedging, diversification, and the use of derivatives (Froot et al. 1993; Hull 2021; Jorion 2006). Investment decision-making is based on project evaluation methods, such as net present value (NPV), internal rate of return (IRR), and the payback period.

With the development of the company, its capital should increase, which should result not only from the increase in loans, shares, or credits, but above all from the net profits of the company (Bień 2016). Financial management is based on the search for and obtaining capital (sources of financing) and the distribution of this capital in assets in such a way as to achieve strategic goals related to maximizing the value of the company (Bień 2016; Głodek 2004). Four groups of decisions with financial consequences leading to an increase in the value of the owner's enterprise can be distinguished (Rutkowski 2003):

1. Operational decisions related to ensuring the current financial balance and ability to pay:

   a. Planning sales profitability.
   b. Establishing a sales program.
   c. Defining the rules for crediting customers.
   d. Determination of the form of repayment of operational liabilities to suppliers.
2. Investment decisions related to capital allocation:
   a. Investments in financial purchases and property, plant, and equipment.
   b. Short-term investments, such as investments in securities.
3. Financial decisions related to the selection of sources of financing of the enterprise, that is:
   a. Raising additional auxiliary equity.
   b. Taking loans or credits.
4. Dividend decisions related to the distribution of the financial result:
   a. Distribution of profit into dividends and the part invested in the company.

Corporate financial management and cyberspace are closely linked. Corporate financial management in cyberspace is closely linked to digital technologies and security. Digitalization is about transforming traditional, analogue processes and data into digital form. This process uses information and communication technologies to automate, optimize, and integrate various areas of economic and social activity. Thanks to digitization, many sectors, including financial management, gain access to modern tools and methods that increase efficiency, precision, and the availability of information. Digitization and the development of information technologies significantly affect the way we manage finances, make investment decisions, or protect data:

1. Digitization of financial processes:
   a. Companies use digital accounting systems, electronic payment platforms, and advanced analytical tools.

   b. ERP systems[2] and fintech solutions enable the automation of financial processes, which improves efficiency and reduces operating costs.
2. Cybersecurity for financial data protection (Raczkowski & Sułkowski 2014):
   a. Financial IT systems are vulnerable to cyberattacks, which can result in data leakage, financial losses, and breaches of data protection regulations.
   b. Enterprises need to invest in security systems such as data encryption, firewalls, and multi-level authorization.
3. Digital payment methods and blockchain technologies:
   a. Companies are increasingly using digital payment methods (e.g., PayPal, Revolut, Google Pay), which affects the speed and security of transactions.
   b. Blockchain and cryptocurrencies enable direct transactions, minimizing commission costs and increasing transparency of settlements.
4. Data analytics and AI:
   a. Advanced algorithms analyze financial data in real time, supporting investment and budget decision-making.
   b. AI helps in forecasting financial liquidity and identifying risks related to financial fraud.
5. Cyberthreats:
   a. Ransomware attacks can lock down access to financial systems, resulting in business paralysis and financial losses.
   b. Cyberattacks, such as phishing, can lead to money extortion and financial fraud.
6. Legal and compliance:
   a. Businesses must comply with international regulations on cybersecurity and data protection.
   b. Anti-money laundering and counter-terrorism financing regulations enforce the use of customer verification procedures.

7. Home office and financial management in the cloud:
   a. The rise of remote work has forced the implementation of cloud systems for financial management, which increases the availability of data, but at the same time raises new cyber threats.
   b. Companies use cloud-based financial systems, which allow for ongoing monitoring of finances and cost optimization.

Digitalization brings many benefits, such as increased efficiency, cost reduction, and improved service quality. At the same time, it poses challenges for companies related to data security, the need to invest in new technologies, and adaptation to changing market conditions (Gajewski et al. 2016).

Financial management is crucial for businesses in the digital era, that is, for the following reasons: Operational efficiency, accuracy and transparency, risk management, availability and flexibility, innovation and competitiveness, regulatory compliance, and better business decisions. Digitization allows for the automation of many financial processes, including accounting, tax settlements, and data analysis. This allows companies to significantly improve operational efficiency by reducing the time and costs associated with manual information processing. Advanced technologies such as AI and machine learning (ML) enable more precise analysis of financial data, leading to greater transparency and accuracy in reporting. This, in turn, plays a key role in making business decisions.

Digitalization enables better risk management by quickly and accurately monitoring financial ratios and identifying potential risks. Technologies such as big data and predictive analytics help companies predict and respond to changing market conditions (Iwanicz-Drozdowska 2021). Moving financial processes to the cloud gives companies greater availability and flexibility. Employees can access financial data from anywhere, at any time, which is especially important in the context of remote work (Iwanicz-Drozdowska 2021). Digitalization opens the door to innovations in financial management, such as blockchain and fintech. Companies that invest in new technologies can gain a competitive advantage by offering more advanced and effective financial services (Duda 2025). Modern technologies help companies meet regulatory requirements by automating compliance processes and ensuring that all financial operations comply with applicable regulations (Duda 2025). With modern analytics tools, businesses can dig deeper into their financial data, enabling them to make more informed business decisions. As a result, this translates into more effective resource management and improved financial results. Each company should create its own financial management model, adapted to both micro and macroeconomic conditions, taking into account the progressing digitization. The areas of the financial management model are:

1. Financial planning:
   a. Financial objectives: Defining operational, tactical, and strategic financial objectives.
   b. Budgeting: Creating budget(s) that take into account all sources of income and expenditure.
   c. Forecasting: Predicting future inflows and expenses based on historical data and trends.
2. Revenue management:
   a. Revenue sources: Identify and optimize different revenue streams.
   b. Revenue strategies: Implementing revenue growth strategies, for example, launching new product(s) or services.
3. Cost management:
   a. Cost control: Monitor and control costs to ensure budget compliance.
   b. Cost optimization: Looking for ways to reduce costs without losing the quality of products or services.

4. Liquidity management:
   a. Financial reserves: Maintaining adequate financial reserves for contingencies.
   b. Cash flow management: Monitoring cash flows to ensure liquidity.
5. Investing:
   a. Investment analysis: Evaluating different investment opportunities, taking into account potential risks and potential rewards.
   b. Portfolio diversification: Investing in different assets to minimize risk.
6. Risk management:
   a. Risk identification: Identification of potential financial risks, that is, exchange rate risk, market changes, credit risk, etc.
   b. Risk management strategies: Implementing strategies to minimize risk, that is, insurance, hedging, etc.
7. Monitoring and control:
   a. Regular audits and controls: Assessment of investment objectives and budget implementation.
   b. Reporting: Creating financial reports that provide information about the current financial situation.
8. Financial education:
   a. Training and development: Investing in the financial education of finance staff to increase financial management knowledge and skills.

## 3.3 Tools Used in Corporate Finance Management

The tools used in the management of the company's finances are illustrated in Table 3.1.

The enterprise management willing to maximize the value of the company must use its strengths and capabilities to

**Table 3.1 Selected Tools Used in the Management of Company Finances**

| *Corporate Finance Management Area* | *Key Tools* |
|---|---|
| Financial analysis | ■ Ratio analysis (profitability, liquidity, debt, efficiency ratios)<br>■ Du Pont analysis (dissecting ROI into its component elements)<br>■ Trend analysis (analysis of financial dynamics over time)<br>■ SWOT analysis in finance (identification of strengths, weaknesses, opportunities, and threats of the company)<br>■ Financial benchmarking (comparison of the company's performance with the competition) |
| Budgeting and financial planning | ■ Operational and financial budgeting<br>■ Capital budgeting (evaluation of investment projects)<br>■ Scenario planning (creating strategies for different market conditions)<br>■ Break-even analysis (determination of minimum sales covering costs)<br>■ Financial forecasting (predictive models for future financial results) |
| Working capital management | ■ Cash flow management<br>■ Management of receivables and liabilities (monitoring of payment dates)<br>■ Inventory optimization (e.g., EOQ model—Economic Order Quantity)<br>■ Cash pooling and netting systems (management of funds in a capital group) |

(*Continued*)

**Table 3.1 (Continued)**

| *Corporate Finance Management Area* | *Key Tools* |
|---|---|
| Assessment and selection of investments | ■ Net present value (NPV)<br>■ Internal rate of return (IRR)<br>■ Payback period<br>■ Sensitivity analysis<br>■ Viable options methods (taking into account decision-making flexibility in investments) |
| Financial risk management | ■ Value at risk (VaR) analysis (assessment of maximum loss at a given confidence level)<br>■ Hedging (hedging financial positions with derivatives)<br>■ Forwards, futures, options, and swaps (management of currency, interest rate, and commodity risks)<br>■ Stress testing and scenario analysis (analysis of the impact of extreme market events |
| IT systems supporting financial management | ■ ERP (enterprise resource planning)—np. SAP, Oracle Financials<br>■ BI (business intelligence)—analytical tools, for example, Power BI, Tableau<br>■ Cash flow management systems—for example, Treasury Management Systems<br>■ Financial modelling platforms—for example, Excel, Python |

*Source:* Own elaboration.

eliminate its weak points. Financial analysis involves comparing the company's performance with the results of other companies in the same industry and assessing trends related to changes in the company's financial situation over time (Brigham & Houston 2015). Financial analysis enables the assessment of the financial situation of a company by analyzing financial ratios, financial statements, and forecasting results (Brigham & Houston 2021; Helfert 2001; Higgins et al. 2023). The analysis of financial statements consists of examining historical financial results and forecasting future ones. Analysis of financial statements enables the assessment of the condition of the company and its operational activities (Siegel & Shim 2011).

"The analysis of the economic efficiency of the company's functioning should be conducted through the prism of finance. (…) As a result, the economic efficiency of the company's operations is fully reflected in its financial situation, the analysis of which should be one of the basic tools for optimizing profits and financial surplus" (Bień 2016).

The main source of financial analysis is financial statements, which are "a synthetic picture of the company's property and financial position as at a specific date and the company's financial results for a given period" (Gabrusewicz 2014). The information contained in the annual financial statements can be the basis for forecasting the level of future profits and dividends, which is why investors are very interested in these documents (Brigham & Houston 2015). Financial statements are the most important reports published by companies for the benefit of shareholders. The first element of the report is a descriptive part, usually in the form of a letter from the president to shareholders, which characterizes the company's operating results for the past year and discusses new projects that will affect the future results of operating activities. The second element of the statement consists of four basic financial documents: A balance sheet which shows what assets the company has at a given time and who claims rights to them, a profit and loss account which shows the revenues obtained by the company and the costs incurred by it in the past period, a cash flow statement which shows the amount of cash with which the company started and ended the year and what actions it took to affect the stocks of this cash, and a statement of changes in equity which illustrates information on changes in individual components of equity (fund) for the current (reporting data) and the previous financial year (comparative data). These documents are interconnected; together they form an accounting picture of the company's financial situation (Antczak 2014; Brigham & Houston 2015).

Budgeting is the process of preparing, approving, executing, and controlling a budget (Szczypa 2008). The budget is a two-sided statement, but the figures on the revenue and expenditure side, that is, the amounts set in the budget, are only indicative; they are a summary of the expected amounts (Walczak and Kowalczyk 2010). Financial planning permits the definition of a financial strategy and control costs in the company (Gitman & Zutter 2019; Horngren et al. 2020; Shim & Siegel 2011). Effective working capital management increases financial liquidity and reduces financial risk (Brealey et al. 2022; Petersen & Rajan 1997; Van Horne & Wachowicz 2015). Evaluation of investment projects allows for effective allocation of capital (Copeland et al. 2015; Damodaran 2012; Ross et al. 2021). Risk management facilitates reducing the impact of adverse market changes on the company's finances (Froot et al. 1993; Hull 2021; Jorion 2006). Digital technologies support financial analysis and capital management (Chaffey & White 2010; Laudon & Laudon 2021; Turban et al. 2018).

Maintaining an appropriate level of financial liquidity is one of the biggest problems of financial management faced by the management of enterprises. Financial liquidity, understood as the ability to pay current liabilities, is the basic condition for the survival of a company in the short term. Even profitable companies can fail due to a temporary lack of liquidity (Davues 1993). Hence, liquidity management is becoming one of the key areas of financial management. Liquidity can be analyzed in a static perspective (based on balance sheet ratios, such as current ratio or quick ratio) and a dynamic perspective (based on the cash flow statement).

The most commonly used ratios (Table 3.2) are: Current ratio, fast ratio, cash ratio, as well as the interest coverage ratio (Skowronek-Mielczarek & Leszczyński 2007a, 2007b).

**Table 3.2 Selected Indicators (Description and Method of Calculation)**

| *Indicators* | *Method of Calculation* |
|---|---|
| **Liquidity ratios**<br>■ These allow for determining the company's ability to repay debts with a maturity date of up to 12 months. | |
| Current liquidity ratio<br>(safe index value: 1.2–2.0) | $\frac{\text{current assets}}{\text{short-term liabilities}}$ |
| Increased liquidity ratio<br>(safe index value: 0.8–1.5) | $\frac{\text{current assets} - \text{inventories}}{\text{short-term liabilities}}$ |
| Cash ratio<br>(safe index value: 0.1–0.2) | $\frac{\text{cash}}{\text{short-term liabilities}}$ |
| Interest coverage ratio | $\frac{\text{operating profit}}{\text{interest costs}}$ |
| **Net working capital**<br>■ The negative value of net working capital indicates an unstable financial situation, the solvency of which is at risk, which, in consequence, means that the liquidity of such a company should be assessed negatively.<br>■ The net working capital being higher than zero means that the company does not bear a high risk of liquidity loss, and its ability to settle its current liabilities is unaffected.<br>■ A positive value of net working capital ensures the smooth operation of the company. | |
| ■ In financial (capital) terms | (equity + long-term external capital) – fixed assets |
| ■ In terms of the balance sheet (accounting) | current assets – short-term liabilities |

(*Continued*)

**Table 3.2 (Continued)**

| *Indicators* | *Method of Calculation* |
|---|---|
| **Activity ratios**[a] ■ These inform about the extent to which the company uses its assets efficiently. | |
| Days sales outstanding | $\frac{\text{average amount of receivables x 365}}{\text{sales revenues}}$ |
| Average period of cover | $\frac{\text{average amount of inventories x 365}}{\text{sales revenues}}$ |
| Days payable outstanding | $\frac{\text{average amount of liabilities x 365}}{\text{sales revenues}}$ |
| Operating cycle | inventory turnover + days of sales outstanding |
| Cash conversion cycle | operating cycle – days of payables outstanding |
| **Debt ratios** ■ These inform about how the company finances its assets and about the capabilities of the company in the area of long-term debt repayment. | |
| Total debt ratio (safe index value: 0.57–0.67) | $\frac{\text{total liabilities}}{\text{total assets}}$ |
| Debt-to-equity ratio (safe index value: 1.0–3.0) | $\frac{\text{total liabilities}}{\text{equity}}$ |
| Long-term debt ratio (safe index value: 0.5–1.0) | $\frac{\text{long – term liabilities}}{\text{equity}}$ |
| **Profitability ratios** ■ These inform about the profitability of the company's operating cash flow. The following relationship should be maintained in a well-functioning company: The return on equity ratio should be higher than the return on assets ratio, which should be higher than the return on sales ratio, that is, ROE > ROA > ROS. | |

(*Continued*)

**Table 3.2 (Continued)**

| *Indicators* | *Method of Calculation* |
|---|---|
| Return on equity (ROE) | $\frac{\text{net profit}}{\text{equity}}$ |
| Return on assets (ROA) | $\frac{\text{net profit}}{\text{total assets}}$ |
| Return On sales (ROS) | $\frac{\text{net profit}}{\text{sales revenues}}$ |
| Return on investment (ROI) | $\frac{\text{operating profit}}{\text{total assets}}$ |

*Source:* Antczak 2023.

a Cycle indicators calculated over the cycle duration of 365 days (year). The average state of receivables, liabilities, and inventories is calculated as the arithmetic mean of the item value from the opening and closing balance sheets.

Excess liquidity can indicate untapped investment potential, while too low liquidity leads to a loss of confidence from investors and lenders. To manage liquidity, tools such as working capital management policy, credit lines, operating leases, and factoring are used (Gołebiowski & Tłaczała 2020). The analysis of cash flows should cover three areas: Operational, investment, and financial. It is crucial to maintain positive operating cash flows that allow self-financing and reinvestment of profits (Nowak 2016). Liquidity management is also of strategic importance in terms of the ability to invest and expand in the market.

When analyzing financial liquidity, it is worth taking into account its connections with various ratios (Pomykalska & Pomykalski 2020):

1. Performance indicators—they are used to assess the efficiency of resource use. The level of financial liquidity depends on working capital, which is shaped by the company's activity in areas such as the receivables

collection cycle, inventory turnover, and payment dates of liabilities. A lack of adequate liquidity can limit a company's ability to make operational decisions.
2. Profitability—it determines the ability of a company (or its resources) to generate profit. A company achieving high profitability can generate positive cash flows, which at the same time have a positive impact on the level of liquidity ratios. Good liquidity may enable the absorption of liabilities, which can affect further development and increase profitability.
3. Debt—it determines the degree of dependence of the company on foreign capital and its ability to pay its liabilities on time. Financial liquidity determines the possibility of incurring new liabilities and shaping the capital structure. Funding decisions have a direct impact on liquidity ratios, especially in the context of short-term liabilities.

Effective management of working capital plays an important role in shaping the financial stability and adaptability of the company. Working capital is the difference between current assets and current liabilities. Its optimization allows not only for maintaining liquidity but also for the effective use of financial resources (Dębski 2013; Gitman & Zutter 2012).

Current assets include mainly inventories, receivables, and cash. Proper management of each of these elements shortens the operating cycle and improves financial efficiency. Companies can use different strategies: Conservative, moderate, and aggressive—each of them is associated with a different level of risk and expected rate of return (Brealey et al. 2014). Inventory management is about optimizing an inventory investment. The level of optimal inventory varies from industry to industry and even among companies operating in the same sector. An effective inventory management policy reduces inventory levels at all stages of production while maintaining efficiency. This approach increases the company's revenues and improves cash flow. Keeping inventory levels low and lead times short increases the company's agility, allowing the company's management to respond immediately to changing economic conditions (Siegel & Shim 2011).

Receivables management should include not only the control of the timeliness of repayments, but also the assessment of the credit risk of contractors. In the case of inventories, it is important to balance the minimum level (reduction of storage costs) with ensuring the continuity of production and sales (Watson & Head 2016). Effective management of receivables affects the profitability of the company and the amount of its cash flows. It is important to take into account the two stages preceding the actual occurrence of the receivables, that is, the invoicing period and the invoices expected to be received (Siegel & Shim, 2011).

By reducing borrowing costs and improving the cash conversion cycle, working capital impacts profitability. Effective management of working capital results in higher operational flexibility and a better negotiating position with the company's financial partners.

Maintaining the company's ability to pay its liabilities is a key aspect of its operation, both in the short and long term. Both excess liquidity and its shortage can have negative consequences. Excess liquidity may suggest a lack of investment activities, while a lack of liquidity may lead to insolvency and, consequently, to the collapse of the company. Effective working capital management contributes to both increasing profitability and reducing the risk of cash shortages. Working capital, defined as the difference between current assets and current liabilities, requires optimal control of both of these categories. An important aspect is to take into account the source of financing the wealth and the inverse proportional relationship between profitability and risk. Shifting cash from fixed assets to current assets reduces liquidity risk, increasing the ability to obtain short-term financing and the overall flexibility of the company. This allows you to adjust the size of current assets to changes in the level of sales.

The use of long-term debt instead of short-term debt reduces the risk of losing financial liquidity, but it is associated with a higher cost of capital resulting from the uncertainty of the company's development in the long term. Higher financing costs reduce profitability (Siegel & Shim, 2011).

Effective management requires simple and understandable quantified goals of activities for all the participants in the enterprise. Defining the basic goal of the company is one of the main elements of its management (Grabowska 2023). From the point of view of owners who have given up their current consumption and invested their funds in the activities of a business entity, the primary goal of the company's operation should focus on maximizing the wealth of the owners in the long term (Grabowska 2023). Maximizing the value for owners is reflected in the management of the company's financial liquidity, that is, maintaining at an optimal level for the business entity assets that can be easily converted into cash, including cash and securities (Wędzki 2003). It is the company's ability to generate cash flows that will enable timely payment of due liabilities and, at the same time, cover unexpected expenses, while the purpose of liquidity management is to maximize these flows in such a way as to maximize value for owners.

Maximizing value for the owner is expressed in the pursuit of:

- Maximizing profit or minimizing costs.
- Maintaining a minimum level of cash.
- Maintaining a minimum level of inventory.
- Meeting the target value of liquidity ratios.
- Maintaining the target share of current liabilities in assets.
- Maintaining target payables coverage (Grabowska 2023).

Profit is the result of the company's achievements and is a source of financing for its development, but it is liquidity that determines the real possibilities of this financing. It forms the basis for ensuring profitability in the future. Maintaining liquidity is treated as a strict side condition of profitability, the failure to comply with which leads to the elimination of the participant from the market game. The pursuit of profitability must be pursued as part of liquidity security. Profitability does not guarantee liquidity, just as the lack of profitability does not necessarily mean problems with the current settlement of liabilities (Grabowska 2023).

It is necessary to develop a strategy that is a kind of compromise: Maintaining an appropriate level of financial liquidity and striving to achieve profit. A higher level of liquidity means having a higher stock of assets that do not generate profit and using more stable, but more expensive forms of financing. Reconciling your short-term and long-term goals allows you to determine the optimal combination of income and risk (Waśniewski & Skoczylas 2004).

Corporate financial management is the process of making decisions about the acquisition, allocation, and control of funds. The main goal is to maximize the market value of the company, which translates into the interest of owners, investors, and broadly understood stakeholders (Ross et al. 2021; Van Horne & Wachowicz 2008). Achieving this goal requires the achievement of intermediate goals, such as ensuring liquidity, profitability, solvency, and operational efficiency. Financial management includes both investment (capital allocation) and financial (financing acquisition) decisions. Investment decisions include the evaluation of investment projects using NPV, IRR, and the payback period (Higgins 2012). Financial management functions include financial planning, financial analysis, budget implementation, control, and strategic decision-making. It is also important to take into account the time value of money and investment risk—the higher the risk, the higher the expected rate of return should be (Brigham & Daves 2020).

Modern financial management also requires monitoring of the external environment, including changes in monetary and tax policy and exchange rate fluctuations. Sustainable development and ESG reporting, which affect the company's market value and access to capital, are becoming increasingly important (Fabozzi & Peterson Drake 2009).

The Chief Financial Officer (CFO) plays a key role in managing a company's finances. The CFO should first be equipped with the ability to use various types of financial management instruments that work mainly to take into account the time value of money and the ability to estimate the degree of risk when making financial decisions (Dębski 2013). The primary goal of the company's management should be to maximize the value of shares in the long term, that is, the internal value of the company expressed in the long-term average rating of the shares (Brigham & Houston 2015). The primary tasks of the CFO are as follows:

1. Ensuring that the accounting system provides reliable data that serve as the foundation for internal business decisions and the basis for investors' decisions.
2. Guaranteeing the proper financing of the company's activities.
3. Evaluation of the activities of individual operating units and coordination of financial activities.
4. Analysis of proposed capital expenditures in terms of the increase in the value of the company.
5. Monitoring expenses and revenues and optimizing costs for active management of financial resources.
6. Conducting regular internal audits to ensure compliance with regulations and financial standards.
7. Identification and management of financial risk, including exchange rate and interest rate risk.
8. Coordination of financial activities with other departments of the company.
9. Maintaining relationships with investors and financial partners.
10. Developing a financial strategy and policy to support the company's business objectives and ensure its financial stability.

Effective company management necessitates the establishment and continuous enhancement of a well-functioning controlling department or controller. The responsibilities of a controller in business management are constantly evolving, primarily due to the environment in which the company operates. Environments can be categorized as stable, changeable, or turbulent. Depending on the type of environment in which the entity operates, three model profiles of the controller can be identified: Recorder, navigator, and innovator. Controller profiles based on environment type (Czubakowska 1995):

1. Recorder (stable environment):
   a. Providing data on past economic processes.
   b. Linking to financial accounting and traditional cost accounting.
   c. Using information from financial statements.
   d. Not participating in the decision-making process.
2. Navigator (variable environment):
   a. Integrating planning with control.
   b. Comparing actual and planned figures.
   c. Preventing possible mistakes.
   d. Eliminating deviations in the present and future tense.
   e. Participating in the decision-making process.
3. Innovator (turbulent environment):
   a. Quickly orienting to changes taking place.
   b. Engaging in vigorous innovation activities.
   c. Improving solutions within the adopted economic system.
   d. Applying modern solutions in financial and management accounting.
   e. Participating in management.

The role of the CFO can be integrated with that of the controller. In the future, the CFO's responsibilities will evolve further. The CFO will not only act as the custodian of the company's finances but also:

- Lead digital transformation within the finance sector.
- Design and implement sustainable development strategies.
- Serve as the chief advisor for strategic risk management.
- Initiate financial innovations, including the adoption of fintech and blockchain solutions.

A modern CFO will combine deep financial knowledge with technological, strategic, and social competencies.

## 3.4 AI-Based Tools for Corporate Finance Management

AI is a broad scientific discipline in which issues from computer science, statistics, mathematics, humanities, philosophy, social sciences, and management intersect. AI aims to develop such computer systems and machines that typically require the effort of the human mind (Karski 2022). Russell and Norvig define AI as:

> the science of algorithmics, fuzzy logic, evolutionary computing, neural networks, artificial life, and robotics. Artificial intelligence is a branch of computer science that aims to study the rules governing intelligent human behavior, create formal models of this behavior, and as a result, develop computer programs that simulate these behaviors.
> (Russell & Norvig 2003)

According to R. Bellman, "AI is the process of automating certain activities, such as decision-making and learning, that mimic human intelligence" (Bellman 1978). Given the definitions according to the Oxford English Dictionary, AI is "the theory and development of computer systems capable of performing tasks that normally require human intelligence" (Burgess 2024). AIs are computer systems that mimic human intelligence by analyzing data, recognizing patterns, predicting outcomes, and making decisions. AI technologies include machine learning (ML), deep learning (DL), and natural language processing (NLP). Thanks to these solutions, it is possible to automatically identify dependencies, analyze data, and optimize operational activities (Ziółkowska 2023). Generative AI is an advanced AI model capable of creating new content based on the data provided. In the context of corporate finance, GenAI is used in data analysis, trend forecasting, and automation of financial processes (Prędkiewicz & Biegun 2024).

AI is playing an increasingly important role in corporate financial management, enabling the automation of processes, improving efficiency, and increasing the accuracy of financial analysis. The introduction of AI technology affects strategic decision-making, cost optimization, and risk protection. Areas of financial management where AI-based tools can be used (Hilpisch 2022; Nowakowski 2023; Szpringer 2024):

1. Automation of financial processes:
   a. AI streamlines day-to-day financial operations such as accounting, invoicing, payment analysis, and cash flow management.
   b. RPA (robotic process automation) systems eliminate human error, reduce operational costs, and speed up data processing.
2. Financial forecasting and data analysis:
   a. AI algorithms analyze historical and current data, providing forecasts on revenues, costs, and financial liquidity.
   b. AI improves budget management, predicts financial crises, and optimizes investment strategies.
3. Financial fraud detection:
   a. AI identifies suspicious transactions and patterns characteristic of financial fraud, such as money laundering and credit fraud.

   b. AI systems used by banks and financial institutions analyze big data in real time, blocking suspicious operations.
4. Optimize investment decisions:
   a. AI algorithms support the management of investment portfolios by providing recommendations on how to buy or sell assets.
   b. AI-driven trading allows you to make investment decisions in fractions of a second, minimizing the risk of losses.
5. Personalization of financial services:
   a. AI enables the customization of financial offers to the individual needs of customers and businesses by analyzing their behavior, spending, and preferences.
   b. Companies can use intelligent financial advice (chatbots, robo-advisors) to optimize their finances.
6. Financial risk management:
   a. AI systems analyze credit, liquidity, and market risks, helping to make strategic financial decisions.
   b. Thanks to big data analytics, companies can react faster to changes in the market and avoid unfavorable financial situations.
7. Cybersecurity in finance:
   a. AI detects and responds to cyber threats related to financial management, that is, hacking attacks on accounting and banking systems.
   b. ML helps to identify unusual user activity and take preventive action.
8. Cost and savings analysis:
   a. AI algorithms support the optimization of operating costs by analyzing expenses and detecting inefficiencies in the budget.
   b. AI and ML can suggest alternative financial strategies to reduce the cost of doing business.

9. Supporting compliance and reporting:
   a. AI supports compliance with legal regulations such as GDPR (General Data Protection Regulation) or AML (Anti-Money Laundering) by automating audits and financial reports.
   b. Generate financial reports in real-time, making it easier to manage internal control.

Table 3.3 characterizes selected tools based on AI that can be used in corporate finance management in the following areas: Financial planning and analysis, investment advisory and portfolio management, data analysis and market research, accounting automation, security and risk management, financial services, analytical tools, and reporting.

AI-based tools for managing corporate finances were searched for using ChatGPT and are presented in Table 3.3, which was prepared by the company.

**Table 3.3 AI-Based Tools for Corporate Finance Management**

| *Financial Management Area* | *AI-Powered Tools* |
|---|---|
| Financial planning and analysis | ■ Adaptive Insights AI (Workday Adaptive Planning): A cloud-based financial planning and analytics solution that enables teams to create budgets, forecasts, and reports.<br>■ Anaplan AI: A scenario planning and analytics platform that uses AI to optimize decision-making in finance, operations, and other areas.<br>■ Excel: A Microsoft spreadsheet tool used for financial management, data analysis, and reporting. |

*(Continued)*

**Table 3.3 (Continued)**

| *Financial Management Area* | *AI-Powered Tools* |
|---|---|
| Investment advice and portfolio management | ■ AI-driven robo-advisors: Automated financial advisory platforms that use AI algorithms to manage investment portfolios based on clients' preferences and risk tolerance.<br>■ Betterment AI: One of the leading robo-advisors, offering automated investment services using algorithm-based strategies.<br>■ Wealthfront AI: A robo-advisory platform that uses algorithms for investment management and financial planning.<br>■ Kavout: An AI-powered investment platform that analyses market data to identify investment opportunities.<br>■ Numerai AI: A hedge fund using AI-based predictive models to manage an investment portfolio. |
| Data analysis and market research | ■ AlphaSense: A platform that uses AI to search and analyze financial documents, reports, and transcripts to gain market insights.<br>■ BloombergGPT: An AI language model specializing in natural language processing tasks in the field of finance. |

(*Continued*)

**Table 3.3 (Continued)**

| *Financial Management Area* | *AI-Powered Tools* |
|---|---|
| Accounting automation | ■ BlackLine AI: It offers solutions for automating financial and accounting processes, using AI for data analysis and anomaly detection.<br>■ Botkeeper: Accounting automation platform for accounting offices, combining AI with accountant support to streamline processes.<br>■ Rossum AI: A financial document automation tool that uses AI to extract data from invoices and other documents.<br>■ Vic.ai: An AI platform for automating accounting processes such as invoice processing and expense management. |
| Security and risk management | ■ Darktrace AI: An AI-based cybersecurity solution that monitors networks to detect and respond to threats in real time.<br>■ FICO Falcon Fraud Manager: A system that detects and prevents fraud in payment transactions, using advanced analytics and predictive models.<br>■ ZestFinance: A platform that uses AI to assess credit risk, analyzing data to predict customers' creditworthiness. |

(*Continued*)

**Table 3.3 (Continued)**

| *Financial Management Area* | *AI-Powered Tools* |
|---|---|
| AI-powered financial services | ■ IBM Watson Financial Services: AI toolkit for financial data analytics, risk management, and compliance.<br>■ Kyriba AI: Working capital management platform, using AI for cash flow forecasting and financial risk management.<br>■ HighRadius: An AI-based solution for automating accounts receivable and payable management processes.<br>■ Tesorio AI: A cash flow management platform that uses AI to forecast and optimize liquidity. |
| Analytics and reporting | ■ Power BI: Microsoft's data analysis and visualization tool used in financial reporting.<br>■ Tableau + AI: A data visualization platform that integrates AI capabilities for advanced analysis and presentation of financial data. |

*Source:* Own elaboration.

AI enables the automation of routine tasks such as invoice processing, reporting, or expense analysis, leading to increased operational efficiency (Walicka & Czemiel-Grzybowska 2023). Benefits of automating financial processes include:

1. Increased efficiency—automation speeds up the processing of financial data and reduces the time it takes to complete routine tasks.
2. Error reduction—automated systems reduce the risk of human error, improving the accuracy of financial information.

3. Cost savings—automation reduces operational costs by eliminating manual data processing and reducing the need for human resources.
4. Improved regulatory compliance—automated systems track changes to regulations, ensuring compliance with regulations and avoiding fines.
5. Faster report generation—automation enables faster and more accurate preparation of financial reports, supporting informed business decisions.

Automation of financial processes brings many benefits that revolutionize financial management in companies. With modern technologies, businesses can simplify repetitive tasks and focus on strategic activities.

Examples of financial process automation applications include automatic invoice posting, automatic tax settlements, monitoring of operating costs, budget management, and forecasting.

AI and ML have great potential to analyze financial data in real time, identify patterns, and forecast financial performance. Examples of practical use of AI and ML are (Adaboina 2024; Babor 2025; Ćwiertniak 2024; Kumar 2025; Prędkiewicz & Biegun 2024; Wasserbacher & Spindler 2021):

1. Real-time financial data analysis:
   a. Automation of data collection—AI allows for the automatic acquisition of financial data from various sources, such as banking systems, financial markets, or customer transactions. This makes the data collection process fast and efficient.
   b. Processing big data—ML algorithms make it possible to process huge amounts of data in real-time. They allow for quick data analysis, identification of key information, and detection of patterns.

2. Pattern identification:
    a. Pattern recognition—ML algorithms, trained on historical data, identify recurring patterns. An example is the detection of correlations between stock prices, economic indicators, and customer behavior.
    b. Behavioral analysis—ML helps to analyze customer behavior, such as spending patterns or investment preferences, which leads to the creation of personalized financial products. Thanks to clustering algorithms, it is possible to group customers by transaction history to tailor offers to specific demographics.
3. Predicting future financial performance:
    a. Predictive modelling—AI uses predictive models such as linear regression, decision trees, or neural networks to predict future financial performance based on historical data. It is possible to forecast changes in stock prices, market trends, or the financial results of companies.
    b. Dynamic trend detection—unsupervised learning algorithms, such as principal component analysis (PCA), identify subtle trends not seen with traditional analysis methods. For example, hedge funds use ML to predict price movements by examining correlations between seemingly unrelated factors.

Despite the numerous benefits, the implementation of GenAI comes with challenges such as integration with existing systems, ethical issues, and the need for appropriate competencies among employees. The future points to the increasing integration of GenAI in financial processes, which may lead to the transformation of business models (Ćwiertniak 2024; Walicka & Czemiel-Grzybowska 2023).

Neilson (2023) and Romanko, Narayan, and Kwon (2023) emphasize the need for a cautious approach to the implementation of the ChatGPT bot in finance. Challenges such as regulation and the risk of generating erroneous recommendations ("AI hallucinations") require the use of mechanisms for overseeing and validating the results generated by AI to ensure their compliance with applicable standards and user expectations. Hybrid models combining AI capabilities with human expertise can offer the most effective solutions to fully exploit the potential of ChatGPT applications in corporate finance.

## 3.5 The Future of Financial Management

Financial management is evolving at a rapid pace, with new technologies and innovations significantly influencing the way businesses manage their financial resources (Table 3.4). In the future, AI systems will not only support financial analysts but also independently recommend investment strategies, manage asset portfolios, and identify red flags of liquidity or profitability threats. Automation of financial processes will eliminate routine accounting, auditing, and reporting activities, increasing efficiency and reducing the risk of human error. In the digital environment, the role of scenario-based financial planning and flexible budgeting, enabling a quick response to changing market conditions, will increase. In the coming decades, financial management will have to integrate ESG (Environmental, Social, Governance) criteria even more strongly with traditional financial indicators. Companies that successfully integrate ESG aspects into their financial strategy are expected to achieve a lower cost of capital, higher investor loyalty, and better long-term performance.

Companies that successfully adapt to change will not only gain a competitive advantage but also increase their resilience to market risks and strengthen their value in the eyes of investors, customers, and society. Three scenarios for the future of corporate financial management can be identified (Table 3.5):

**Table 3.4 Future Trends in the Financial Management of the Enterprise**

| *Trend* | *Characteristics* | *Potential Impact on Businesses* |
|---|---|---|
| Digitization of finance and automation | ■ Automation of financial processes, the use of AI, blockchain, and big data | ■ Increase in operational efficiency, shortening reporting time, and reducing costs |
| Development of responsible finance (ESG) | ■ Integration of environmental, social, and governance aspects in financial management | ■ Lower cost of capital, more attractive to investors, stronger reputation |
| Advanced analytics and predictive models | ■ Use of big data and advanced algorithms in financial forecasting and planning | ■ Better anticipation of risks and opportunities, more dynamic allocation of resources |
| A new role for the CFO | ■ CFO as a digital transformation leader, responsible for ESG strategy and strategic risk management | ■ Growing importance of the finance function in the management of the entire company |
| Behavioural finance and decision psychology | ■ Acknowledging the impact of emotions and cognitive biases on financial decisions | ■ Better alignment of financial policies with real-world decision-maker behavior |
| Adapting to the digital economy | ■ New revenue models, change in the structure of assets and liabilities | ■ The need for dynamic liquidity management and flexible budgeting |

*Source:* Own elaboration.

**Table 3.5 Scenarios for the Future of Corporate Finance Management**

| *Criterion* | *Optimistic Scenario* | *Realistic Scenario* | *Pessimistic Scenario* |
|---|---|---|---|
| Technology | ■ Full integration of AI, automation, and analytics | ■ Partial implementation of new technologies | ■ Limited or no technology implementations |
| ESG | ■ Holistic adaptation of ESG principles | ■ Selective deployment of elements of ESG | ■ Lack of ESG integration, risk of exclusion |
| Risk management | ■ Dynamic, predictive risk management | ■ Standard risk management | ■ Reactive risk management, increased risks |
| The role of the CFO | ■ Digital transformation and strategy leader | ■ Gradually expanding the role of the CFO | ■ CFO limited to traditional functions |
| Financial results | ■ Increase in efficiency and company value | ■ Stabilization of results with moderate growth | ■ Decrease in profitability and increase in the risk of bankruptcy |
| Market condition | ■ Strong competitive position | ■ Staying on the market | ■ Loss of position, risk of marginalization |

*Source*: Own elaboration

1. An optimistic scenario, meaning digital transformation as a catalyst for development.
2. A realistic scenario, meaning gradual evolution and adaptation.
3. A pessimistic scenario, indicating the risk of stagnation and an increase in threats.

In the optimistic scenario, companies effectively implement new financial technologies, integrate advanced analytics, as well as a full ESG strategy in their operations and finance. Corporate finance becomes the center of innovation, and risk and resource management are dynamic, flexible, and predictive. Companies achieve higher efficiency, minimize risk, raise cheaper capital, and build strong, lasting relationships with investors and society.

In the realistic scenario, the adoption of new ESG technologies and practices is gradual, with the pace of change depending on the size, sector, and resources of the company. Not all companies will be able to fully exploit the potential of AI or predictive analytics, but most will adapt their financial management models to new market requirements.

In the pessimistic scenario, some companies will not adapt to dynamic technological and social changes (Banaszek & Fimińska-Banaszyk 2017). Lack of investment in new technologies, ignoring ESG risks, and incompetent data management will result in increased financing costs (McCullough 2024), loss of competitiveness, and increased vulnerability to crises.

## Notes

1 Expense and cost are synonymous concepts.

2 An ERP (Enterprise Resource Planning) system is a software for comprehensive business management.

## References

Adaboina, S. R. (2024). AI and ML in fraud detection https://www.sciencetimes.com/articles/60131/20241216/ai-ml-fraud-detection.htm

Antczak, J. (2014). Controlling w przedsiębiorstwie w: Wiśniewska, A. M., & Antczak, J. (eds.), *Controlling a strategie rozwoje MSP z województwa mazowieckiego*. Warszawa: Akademia Finansów i Biznesu Vistula.

Antczak, J. (2020). *Zarządzanie przedsiębiorstwem w cyberprzestrzeni*. Warszawa: Akademia Sztuki Wojennej.

Antczak, J. (2023). Finance management in a turbulent environment on the example of a company operating in the video games industry. Silesian University of Technology Publishing House Scientific Papers of Silesian University of Technology, Organization and Management Series No. 168. http://dx.doi.org/10.29119/1641-3466.2023.168.1

Antczak, J. (2024). *Zarządzaniecyberbezpieczeństwem w przedsiębiorstwie doświadczenia wybranych państw Unii Europejskiej*. Warszawa: Difin.

Arnold, G. (2019). *Corporate financial management*. Harlow: Pearson.

Babor, B. (2025). How does AI recognize patterns and make predictions? https://www.stack-ai.com/articles/how-does-ai-recognize-patterns-and-make-predictions

Baker, M., & Wurgler, J. (2002). Market timing and capital structure. *The Journal of Finance*, 57(1), 1–32.

Banaszek, P., & Fimińska-Banaszyk, R. (2017). Cele społeczne i systemowe w przedsiębiorstwie, Zeszyty Naukowe Akademii Ekonomicznej w Poznaniu nr 256 Poznań.

Bellman, R. (1978). *An introduction to artificial intelligence*. Reading, MA: Addison-Wesley.

Bień, W. (2016). *Zarządzanie finansami przedsiębiorstwa*. Warszawa: Difin.

Brealey, R. A., Myers, S. C., & Allen, F. (2014). *Principles of corporate finance*. New York: McGraw-Hill Education.

Brealey, R. A., Myers, S. C., & Allen, F. (2022). *Principles of corporate finance*. New York: McGraw-Hill.

Brigham, E. F. (2019). *Financial management: Theory & practice*. Concise by Cengage Cengage Learning.

Brigham, E. F., & Daves, P. R. (2020). *Intermediate financial management*. Concise by Cengage Cengage Learning.

Brigham, E., & Houston, J. (2015). *Zarządzanie finansami*. Warszawa: PWN.

Brigham, E. F., & Houston, J. F. (2021). *Fundamentals of financial management*. Concise by Cengage Cengage Learning.

Burgess, A. (2024). *The executive guide to artificial intelligence: Cutting through the hype - How to get the most from AI in your organization*. London: Palgrave Macmillan.

Chaffey D. & White S. (2010). *Business information management: Improving performance using information systems*. Harlow: Pearson Education.

Copeland, T., Koller, T., & Murrin, J. (2015). *Valuation: Measuring and managing the value of companies*. New York: McKinsey & Company.

Ćwiertniak, R. (2024). Ludzie i boty sztucznej inteligencji w nowoczesnych projektach. *Zeszyty Naukowe Szkoły Głównej Handlowej w Warszawie*, 199, 79–94.

Czekaj, J., & Ziębicki, B. (red.) (2021). *Współczesne zarządzanie. Koncepcje, metody, systemy*. Kraków: Wydawnictwo Uniwersytetu Ekonomicznego w Krakowie.

Czubakowska, K. (1995). *Funkcje i zadania controllera w przedsiębiorstwie, Prace Naukowe AE we Wrocławiu nr 698*, Wrocław: Wrocław University of Economics.

Damodaran, A. (2012). *Investment valuation: Tools and techniques for determining the value of any asset*. Hoboken: Wiley.

Davues, D. (1993). *Sztuka zarządzania finansami*. Warszawa-Londyn: McGraw Hill.

Dębski, W. (2013). *Teoretyczne i praktyczne aspekty zarządzania finansami przedsiębiorstwa*. Warszawa: Wydawnictwo Naukowe PWN.

Demirgüç-Kunt, A., & Maksimovic, V. (1998). Law, finance, and firm growth. *The Journal of Finance*, 53(6), 2107–2137.

Duda, R. (2025). Jakie innowacje w bankowości zmieniają sposób zarządzania finansami osobistymi? https://www.100pomyslownabiznes.eu/jakie-innowacje-w-bankowosci-zmieniaja-sposob-zarzadzania-finansami-osobistymi/

Fabozzi, F. J., & Drake, P. P. (2009). *Finance: Capital markets, financial management, and investment management*. Hoboken: Wiley.

Froot, K. A., Scharfstein, D. S., & Stein, J. C. (1993). Risk management: Coordinating corporate investment and financing policies. *The Journal of Finance*, 48(5), 1629–1658.

Gabrusewicz, W. (2014). *Analiza finansowa przedsiębiorstwa. Teoria i zastosowanie*. Warszawa: Polskie Wydawnictwo Ekonomiczne.

Gajewski, J., Paprocki, W., & Pieriegud, J. (red.) (2016). *Cyfryzacja gospodarki i społeczeństwa – szanse i wyzwania dla sektorów infrastrukturalnych*. Gdańsk: Instytut Badań nad Gospodarką Rynkową – Gdańska Akademia Bankowa.

Gitman, L. J., & Zutter, C. J. (2012). *Principles of managerial finance*. Harlow: Pearson Education.

Gitman, L. J., & Zutter, C. J. (2019). *Principles of managerial finance*. Harlow: Pearson.

Głodek, Z. (2004). *Zarządzanie finansami przedsiębiorstw*. Warszawa: Polskie Wydawnictwo Ekonomiczne.

Gołebiowski, G., & Tłaczała, A. (2020). *Analiza finansowa przedsiębiorstwa*. Warszawa: Difin.

Grabowska, M. (2023). *Zarządzanie płynnością finansową przedsiębiorstw*. Warszawa: CeDeWu.

Graham, J. R., & Harvey, C. R. (2001). The theory and practice of corporate finance: Evidence from the field. *Journal of Financial Economics*, 60(2–3), 187–243.

Helfert, E. A. (2001). *Financial analysis: Tools and techniques*. New York: McGraw-Hill.

Higgins, R. C. (2012). *Analysis for financial management*. New York: McGraw-Hill Education.

Higgins, R. C., Koski, J., & Mitton, T. (2023). *Analysis for financial management*. New York: McGraw-Hill.

Hilpisch, Y. (2022). *Sztuczna inteligencja w finansach. Używaj języka Python do projektowania i wdrażania algorytmów AI*. Gliwice: Helion.

Horngren, C. T., Datar, S. M., & Rajan, M. (2020). *Cost accounting: A managerial emphasis*. Harlow: Pearson.

Hull, J. C. (2021). *Options, futures, and other derivatives*. Harlow: Pearson.

Iwanicz-Drozdowska, M. (2021). *Zarządzanie finansowe bankiem w erze cyfrowej*. Warszawa: Polskie Wydawnictwo Ekonomiczne.

Jorion, P. (2006). *Value at risk: The new benchmark for managing financial risk*. New York: McGraw-Hill.

Karski, K. (2022). Wybrane zastosowania sztucznej inteligencji w medycynie. *Management and Quality – Zarządzanie I Jakość*, 4(4).
Kumar, A. (2025). How AI and edge computing are transforming real-time financial planning. https://www.analyticsinsight.net/artificial-intelligence/how-ai-and-edge-computing-are-transforming-real-time-financial-planning
Laudon K. C. & Laudon P. (2021). *Management information systems: Managing the digital firm*. Harlow: Pearson Higher Education.
McCullough, J. (2024). The CFO's evolving playbook: Strategic priorities for 2025 and beyond. https://www.forbes.com/sites/jackmccullough/2024/12/12/the-cfos-evolving-playbook-strategic-priorities-for-2025-and-beyond/
McKinsey & Company. (2023). *State of AI in financial services*. New York: McKinsey & Company.
Modigliani, F., & Miller, M. H. (1958). The cost of capital, corporation finance, and the theory of investment. *The American Economic Review*, 48(3), 261–297.
Myers, S. C. (1984). The capital structure puzzle. *The Journal of Finance*, 39(3), 575–592.
Neilson, B. (2023). Artificial intelligence authoring financial recommendations: Comparative Australian evidence. *Journal of Financial Regulation*, 9(2), 249–257.
Nowak, E. (2016). *Analiza sprawozdań finansowych*. Warszawa: PWE.
Nowakowski, M. (2023). *Sztuczna inteligencja. Praktyczny przewodnik dla sektora innowacji finansowych*. Warszaw: Wolters Kluwer Polska.
Petersen, M. A., & Rajan, R. G. (1997). Trade credit: Theories and evidence. *The Review of Financial Studies*, 10(3), 661–691.
Pomykalska, B., & Pomykalski, P. (2020). *Analiza finansowa przedsiębiorstwa*. Warszawa: PWN.
Prędkiewicz, K., & Biegun, K. (2024). AI – sztuczna inteligencja w finansach przedsiębiorstw. [in:] Sierpińska M., & Szczepanowski P. (eds.). *Finanse przedsiębiorstw*. Warszawa: PWN.
PwC. (2024). Gotowi na sztuczną inteligencję. https://www.pwc.pl/pl/publikacje/gotowi-na-sztuczna-inteligencje-raport.html
Raczkowski, K., & Sułkowski, Ł. (red.). (2014). *Zarządzanie bezpieczeństwem. Metody i techniki*. Warszawa: Difin.
Romanko, O., Narayan, A., & Kwon, R. H. (2023). ChatGPT-based investment portfolio selection. *Operations Research Forum*, 4(4), 91.

Ross, S. A., Westerfield, R. W., Jordan, B. D., & Gordons, R. (2021). *Fundamentals of corporate finance*. New York: McGraw-Hill.

Russell, S., & Norvig, P. (2003). *Artificial intelligence: A modern approach*, 2nd ed. New Jersey: Prentice Hall.

Rutkowski, A. (2003), *Zarządzanie finansami. Teoria i praktyka*. Warszawa: Polskie Wydawnictwo Ekonomiczne (PWE).

Shim, J. K., & Siegel, J. G. (2011). *Budgeting basics and beyond*. Hoboken: Wiley.

Siegel, J. K., & Shim, J. K. (2011). *Dyrektor finansowy*. Kraków: Dom Wydawniczy ABC.

Skowronek-Mielczarek, A., & Leszczyński, Z. (2007a). *Controlling analiza i monitoring w zarządzaniu przedsiębiorstwem*. Warszawa: Difin.

Skowronek-Mielczarek, A., & Leszczyński, Z. (2007b). *Płynność finansowa w zarządzaniu przedsiębiorstwem*. Warszawa: C.H. Beck.

Szczypa, P. (2008). *Rachunkowość zarządcza*. Warszawa: CeDeWu.

Szpringer, W. (2024). *Sztuczna inteligencja w zarządzaniu*. Warszawa: Regulacja a konkurencja Poltext.

Turban, E., Pollard, C. & Wood, G. (2018). *Information technology for management: On demand strategies for performance, growth and sustainability*. Hoboken: John Wiley & Sons.

Van Horne, J. C., & Wachowicz, J. M. (2008). *Fundamentals of financial management*. Harlow: Pearson Education.

Van Horne, J. C., & Wachowicz, J. M. (2015). *Fundamentals of financial management*. Harlow: Pearson.

Walczak, M., & Kowalczyk, K. (2010). *Rachunkowość i budżetowanie w zarządzaniu finansami gminy*. Warszawa: Difin.

Walicka, M., & Czemiel-Grzybowska, W. (2023). Sztuczna inteligencja w zarządzaniu kapitałem przedsiębiorstwa w dobie Przemysłu 5.0. *Akademia Zarządzania*, 7(4), 109–125.

Waśniewski, T., & Skoczylas, W. (2004). *Teoria i praktyka analizy finansowej przedsiębiorstwa*. Warszawa: Fundacja rozwoju rachunkowości w Polsce.

Wasserbacher, H., & Spindler, M. (2021). Machine learning for financial forecasting, planning and analysis: recent developments and pitfalls. https://www.stack-ai.com/articles/how-does-ai-recognize-patterns-and-make-predictions

Watson, D., & Head, A. (2016). *Corporate finance: Principles and practice*. Harlow: Pearson Education.

Wędzki, D. (2003). *Strategie Płynności Finansowej Przedsiębiorstwa*. Kraków: Oficyna Ekonomiczna.

Zingales, L. (1998). Survival of the fittest or the fattest? Exit and financing in the trucking industry. *The Journal of Finance*, 53(3), 905–938.

Ziółkowska, E. (2023). *Wpływ sztucznej inteligencji na rynek finansowy w procesie podejmowania decyzji ekonomicznych – szanse, wyzwania i rekomendacje, Studia i Prace Kolegium Zarządzania i Finansów* Nr 192 (2023) Wydawca: Szkoła Główna Handlowa w Warszawie, DOI: 10.33119/SIP.2023.192.5

## Websites

https://darktrace.com/
https://numer.ai/
https://powerbi.microsoft.com/
https://rossum.ai/
https://www.alpha-sense.com/
https://www.anaplan.com/platform/intelligence/
https://www.betterment.com/
https://www.blackline.com/why-blackline/blackline-ai/
https://www.bloomberg.com/company/press/bloomberggpt-50-billion-parameter-llm-tuned-finance/
https://www.botkeeper.com/
https://www.fico.com/en/products/fico-falcon-fraud-manager
https://www.highradius.com/
https://www.ibm.com/industries/financial-services
https://www.kavout.com/
https://www.kyriba.com/
https://www.microsoft.com/en-us/microsoft-365/excel
https://www.spglobal.com/en/enterprise/partners/kensho/
https://www.tableau.com/products/artificial-intelligence
https://www.tesorio.ai/
https://www.vic.ai/
https://www.wealthfront.com/explore/collections/46/generative-ai
https://www.workday.com/en-us/products/adaptive-planning/overview.html
https://www.yieldstreet.com/blog/article/ai-robo-advisors/
https://www.zest.ai/

# Chapter 4

# Humanoid Robots in Enterprises

The development of humanoid robots has a rich history that reflects advancements in AI and robotics. Early prototypes, such as WABOT-1 in the 1970s, served as foundational experiments in combining mobility with basic cognitive functions (Kaplan 2016). These early designs inspired later iterations that emphasized social interaction, as seen in Honda's ASIMO, introduced in 2000, which showcased capabilities such as walking, running, and understanding simple commands (Vanderelst & Winfield 2018).

In the 2010s, humanoid robots transitioned from research labs into enterprises. SoftBank Robotics' Pepper, launched in 2014, became a milestone, being the first humanoid robot designed to recognize emotions and interact with customers in retail settings (Kaplan 2016). Similarly, Hanson Robotics' Sophia, with her advanced conversational AI and lifelike expressions, demonstrated the potential for humanoid robots in public relations and advisory roles (Floridi & Cowls 2019; Hanson Robotics[1]). Humanoid robots have found applications across a variety of enterprise domains, highlighting their versatility and effectiveness.

DOI: 10.1201/9781003739364-4

Their application in enterprise management has gained attention due to their potential to transform operational processes, enhance decision-making, and improve overall efficiency. With capabilities that include advanced machine learning, natural language processing, and sensor-based human–robot interaction (HRI), humanoid robots are no longer limited to industrial settings; they are becoming integral to service industries, corporate management, and customer-facing roles (Brynjolfsson & McAfee 2014; Skubis & Mosek 2025).

Humanoid robots are entering the workforce, particularly following Elon Musk's presentation of Tesla's Optimus prototype in 2021, which has intensified global competition in robotics. Many companies, especially in North America and Asia, are heavily investing in humanoid robots, viewing them as the next technological breakthrough. However, despite the rapid advancements, several challenges remain, including technological limitations, business viability, and operational feasibility (Noreils 2024).

The Technical Report on Automation and Robots in Services (Sostero 2020) distinguishes industrial robots, used in automation applications like manufacturing and assembly, from service robots (SRs), which perform non-industrial tasks for humans or equipment. SRs are categorized as professional (e.g., hospital delivery robots, cleaning robots) or personal (e.g., automated wheelchairs, domestic assistant robots). SRs are an advanced evolution of industrial robots, requiring higher autonomy to operate in unstructured environments and interact with humans.

According to Sostero (2020), another type of robot, a social robot, which is a subgroup of SRs, is capable of interacting and communicating with humans, other robots, and the environment. Some SRs can act as social robots (e.g., customer-service bots), but not all social robots fit within the service robot category, especially those designed for personal use. Social robots are designed for HRI (Coeckelbergh 2021; Sharkey & Sharkey 2020; Skubis 2024) to independently interact with people across various contexts using natural, human-like social signals (Vollmer et al. 2018).

The logistics sector is a primary target for humanoid robots due to labor shortages and challenging working conditions. However, Noreils (2024) argues that this perceived shortage is misleading. Rather than an actual lack of workers, the issue stems from low wages and harsh environments, leading to high turnover rates. While improving salaries and working conditions is an alternative, companies prefer automation to maintain profit margins.

China, in particular, has taken a strategic approach, setting ambitious goals for mass production of humanoid robots by 2025 and their widespread economic integration by 2027. Large-scale government funding is accelerating the development of domestic humanoid robot suppliers, fostering intense competition (Noreils 2024).

The significance of humanoid robots in enterprise management lies not only in their ability to improve efficiency but also in their potential to address workforce challenges, such as labor shortages and the need for consistent service quality. For example, humanoid robots like SoftBank's Pepper and Hanson Robotics' Sophia have been employed in customer service and advisory roles, illustrating their practical applications in diverse organizational contexts (Kaplan 2016). However, their usage raises complex ethical questions, including those related to privacy, accountability, transparency, and fairness, necessitating a robust regulatory framework to mitigate risks (Floridi & Cowls 2019; Skubis 2024a).

A human-centric approach to AI emphasizes the importance of aligning technological developments with human values and societal well-being. It ensures that robots augment, rather than replace, human capabilities while safeguarding ethical principles (Skubis et al. 2024). This approach is particularly relevant in light of the European Union's emphasis on responsible AI, as outlined in its AI Act (2024), which prioritizes transparency, accountability, and fairness in AI systems (European Commission 2019, 2021b).

This chapter explores the integration of humanoid robots into enterprise environments, focusing on their autonomy, decision-making capacities, and the ethical implications of their deployment. This analysis highlights the need for a human-centric approach to ensure that their deployment aligns with ethical standards, regulatory requirements, and societal values (European Commission 2021a; the EU AI Act 2024).

## 4.1 The Role of Social and Humanoid Robots in Tourism, Hospitality, and Gastronomy

Social robots, defined as autonomous entities capable of interacting with humans through verbal and non-verbal communication (Breazeal 2003; Fong et al. 2003; Skubis 2024b), are increasingly being adopted to enhance customer experiences and operational efficiency in the tourism, hospitality, and gastronomy industries. Humanoid robots, distinguished by their human-like appearance and behaviors, offer unique opportunities and challenges for the industries (Ivanov & Webster 2019).

The adoption of humanoid robots in hospitality can be analyzed through models such as the Technology Acceptance Model (TAM) (Davis 1989), Unified Theory of Acceptance and Use of Technology (UTAUT) (Venkatesh et al. 2003; Venkatesh et al. 2016), and Service Quality Models (Parasuraman et al. 1988). These models help to understand the determinants of acceptance among both customers and hospitality managers. However, user acceptance is highly influenced by ethical concerns, such as data privacy, fairness in algorithmic decision-making, and transparency of humanoid robot operations.

In hotels, they manage front desk operations, greet guests, assist with check-ins and check-outs, and provide information about hotel amenities, local attractions, and dining options (Ivanov & Webster 2019; Skubis et al. 2024; Tussyadiah & Park 2018). These robots can operate 24/7, offering consistent service without fatigue, which is particularly beneficial during peak seasons or late hours (Murphy et al. 2019).

In restaurants, humanoid robots are used for greeting customers, guiding them to their tables, taking orders, and even serving food. Robots like BellaBot and Cruzr are designed with advanced navigation systems that allow them to move seamlessly around dining areas, avoiding obstacles and interacting politely with patrons (Belanche et al. 2019; Qiu et al. 2020). This improves not only service speed and accuracy but also adds an element of novelty that attracts customers.

Tourism information centers and museums also benefit from humanoid robots that act as interactive guides. These robots can provide multilingual support, answer frequently asked questions, and deliver engaging presentations about exhibits or local heritage sites (Choi et al. 2019; Wirtz et al. 2018). Their ability to adapt content based on visitor preferences enhances the overall tourist experience.

Moreover, humanoid robots contribute to back-of-house operations by managing inventory, processing payments, and handling reservations. This reduces the administrative burden on human staff, allowing them to focus on more complex and personalized guest interactions (Seyitoğlu & Ivanov 2020; Tuomi et al. 2020).

### *4.1.1 Ethical Considerations, Customer Perceptions, and Human Oversight*

Research indicates mixed customer perceptions regarding humanoid robots. While some guests appreciate the novelty, efficiency, and entertainment value (Tussyadiah & Park 2018), others express concerns about the lack of human warmth and personalized service (Lu et al. 2019; Qiu et al. 2020). Factors influencing these perceptions include the robot's anthropomorphism, interactivity, and the context of the service provided (Wirtz et al. 2018). For instance, Belanche et al. (2019) found that customers are more accepting of robots in roles perceived as non-critical to the overall service experience. Customer acceptance of robots is influenced by their level of human-likeness (anthropomorphism), as well as perceived gender, ethnicity, and cultural traits. Additionally, technical design factors like material and size play a role, particularly in minimizing any sense of physical risk for consumers.

Additionally, consumer trust is affected by ethical concerns such as data privacy, bias in AI decision-making, and the transparency of robot functions. The European Union's AI Act emphasizes the necessity of explainability in AI systems, which applies to humanoid robots providing recommendations or handling transactions in hospitality. In order to ensure compliance with AI-related regulations such as the EU AI Act and GDPR, hotels must ensure transparency in data collection, storage, and processing, particularly when robots interact with guests and handle sensitive personal data.

Hotel managers recognize both the potential benefits and limitations of humanoid robots. Ivanov, Seyitoğlu, and Markova (2020) found that managers in Bulgaria viewed robots as suitable for repetitive, dull, and dangerous tasks but preferred human staff for roles requiring emotional intelligence and complex problem-solving. Concerns include high costs, maintenance challenges, and potential impacts on service quality. Furthermore, Murphy et al. (2019) emphasized that managers must consider the integration process carefully to balance technological efficiency with the traditional values of hospitality.

The usage of humanoid robots can lead to increased operational efficiency, cost reductions, and enhanced service consistency (Belanche et al. 2019). However, the impact on perceived service quality is nuanced. While robots can improve efficiency and novelty, they may fall short in delivering personalized and empathetic customer service (Choi et al. 2019). Research by Tussyadiah (2020) suggests that customers' expectations play a critical role in determining their satisfaction with robotic services.

The deployment of humanoid robots in hospitality, tourism, and gastronomy raises ethical issues related to employment, data privacy, and HRIs. Concerns about job displacement are prominent, although some argue that robots complement rather than replace human workers, allowing staff to focus on higher-value tasks (Tuomi et al. 2020), which may, for example, require a problem-solving approach or emotional intelligence (Huang & Rust 2018). Data security and ethical programming of robots are also critical considerations (Murphy et al. 2019). Additionally, Wirtz et al. (2018) highlighted the importance of addressing biases in robot design to ensure inclusive and fair service delivery.

Several key ethical issues must be addressed for sustainable humanoid robot adoption in hospitality:

- Job displacement and workforce ethics: While robots can enhance efficiency, replacing human employees with AI-driven systems raises concerns regarding employment and fair labor practices. The hospitality industry must balance automation with human involvement to ensure ethical workforce management (Tuomi et al. 2020).
- Data privacy and AI transparency: Humanoid robots process guest information, requiring strict adherence to GDPR. Hotels must ensure transparency regarding the purpose of data collection, consent mechanisms, and data protection strategies.
- Algorithmic fairness and bias: AI-driven robots must avoid discriminatory behavior when providing personalized services. Bias in facial recognition and language processing could result in uneven service quality across customer demographics (Murphy et al. 2019).

- Deception and trust: Guests should be aware of when they are interacting with a robot rather than a human. Ethical AI guidelines discourage the intentional design of robots to deceive users (Sharkey & Sharkey 2020).

The AI Act stipulates that AI systems deployed in high-risk contexts, such as autonomous decision-making in financial transactions or guest interactions, require clear human oversight and accountability structures. The hospitality sector must incorporate these safeguards into its robot deployment strategies.

The future of humanoid robots in tourism and hospitality is promising yet contingent on technological advancements, cost reductions, and evolving consumer expectations. The COVID-19 pandemic has accelerated interest in contactless services, positioning robots as valuable assets for ensuring health and safety (Seyitoğlu & Ivanov 2020). Moreover, advancements in AI and machine learning are expected to enhance the capabilities of humanoid robots, making them more adaptable to dynamic hospitality environments (Tussyadiah 2020).

Bowen and Morosan (2018) claimed in 2018 that by 2030, robots are expected to make up around 25% of the hotel industry's workforce, taking over tasks traditionally performed by humans. While AI offers potential benefits, understanding stakeholders' perspectives on its societal and industry-wide impacts is crucial. However, uncertainty remains about whether robots can replicate human warmth and emotional expression to meet customer expectations. It presents both opportunities for new business models and challenges that may lead to the decline of some hotels (Palrão, et al. 2023; Rosete et al. 2020).

Humanoid robots represent a significant innovation in tourism, hospitality, and gastronomy, offering both opportunities and challenges. Their successful implementation requires careful consideration of technological capabilities, customer preferences, ethical implications, and organizational readiness. Ongoing research and practical experimentation will continue to shape their role in the industry.

## *4.1.2 Case Studies of Humanoid Robots in Hospitality*

### *4.1.2.1 Connie Robot*

Connie, the humanoid robot introduced by Hilton Hotels, named after Hilton's founder Conrad Hilton, is the first Watson-enabled robot designed for the hospitality sector. Developed in collaboration with IBM, Connie is stationed at the Hilton McLean in Virginia, where it interacts with guests, assists with inquiries, and enhances the overall customer experience. Connie uses IBM Watson's cognitive computing technology, integrating several AI-powered APIs, including Dialog, Speech to Text, Text to Speech, and Natural Language Classifier. These enable the robot to:

- Greet guests upon arrival.
- Provide information about hotel amenities, services, and operational hours.
- Answer visitor queries in a natural and conversational manner.
- Offer personalized recommendations for local attractions by tapping into WayBlazer's travel domain knowledge.

By continuously interacting with guests, Connie learns and improves its responses over time. Hilton staff can also access logs of guest inquiries and Connie's answers, allowing them to refine services and enhance guest satisfaction. Connie represents Hilton's commitment to innovation, aligning with the company's history of introducing groundbreaking technologies, such as in-room televisions in 1947 and digital check-in services. By integrating AI-driven concierge services, Hilton aims to provide guests with more engaging and efficient experiences (IBM[2]).

Rather than replacing human employees, Connie is designed to work alongside Hilton's staff, complementing their roles by handling routine inquiries and providing instant information. This allows human employees to focus on more complex and personalized interactions (*USA Today Travel*[3]).

IBM Watson's cognitive capabilities enable Connie to continuously develop, reflecting a broader trend in AI adoption within the hospitality sector. The integration of AI-powered SRs like Connie not only enhances customer engagement but also sets the stage for future developments in AI-driven hospitality experiences. Connie is an example of how cognitive computing and robotics can redefine guest interactions, offering a glimpse into the future of AI-assisted travel and accommodation services (Skubis et al. 2024).

#### *4.1.2.2 Pepper*

Pepper, developed by SoftBank Robotics, is a humanoid robot widely used across multiple industries, including retail, healthcare, education, banking, and hospitality. Known for its friendly AI and human-like interactions, Pepper enhances customer experiences by providing information, entertainment, and interactive services (Skubis 2025). In the hospitality sector, Pepper is transforming guest experiences by assisting with various tasks that streamline hotel operations and improve customer engagement.

Key functions in tourism and hospitality include (RobotLab[4]):

- Guest greeting and reception: Pepper welcomes guests, provides check-in assistance, and offers information about hotel amenities and services. It can also notify hotel staff when a visitor arrives, improving efficiency.

- Multilingual assistance: Pepper enhances the guest experience by communicating in multiple languages, ensuring smooth interactions for international travelers.
- Concierge and travel guide: The robot provides recommendations for local attractions, dining, and activities. It can also offer guided tours using scripted or conversation-based approaches.
- Entertainment and engagement: Pepper interacts with guests through fun animations, games, and activities such as fist bumps, air guitar performances, and memory games, increasing guest satisfaction.
- Lead generation and customer interaction: Pepper can collect customer information via touchscreen forms, personalize interactions by recognizing guests, and address them by name.
- Room service and assistance: In some hotels, Pepper assists staff by delivering items to rooms, reducing the workload for human employees.
- Conversational AI and chatbot integration: Using AI-driven natural speech recognition, Pepper can understand and respond naturally to guest inquiries, making interactions more seamless.
- Virtual calls and remote assistance: Guests can initiate video calls through Pepper, connecting with remote hotel staff for additional support.
- Analytics and fleet management: Hotel managers can track Pepper's interactions with guests, monitor frequently asked questions, and manage multiple robots across locations.

Pepper enhances customer service by combining AI-driven interactions with human-like engagement, making hotel stays more efficient and enjoyable. Automating routine tasks allows human staff to focus on delivering high-quality personalized service, setting a new standard for guest experiences in tourism and hospitality.

### *4.1.2.3 Humanoid Robots in Henn-na Hotel*

The Henn-na Hotel in Japan is recognized for its pioneering use of humanoid robots in hospitality, employing them for check-in, concierge services, and guest interactions in multiple languages. While initially seen as a groundbreaking innovation, the hotel's experience revealed the limitations of full automation without human oversight. Many robots, such as in-room assistant "Churi" and dinosaur reception robots, struggled with basic tasks, often frustrating guests rather than enhancing their stay (Skubis et al. 2024).

After four years, more than half of the hotel's 243 robots were dismissed, as they created additional work for human staff instead of reducing it. Issues included the inability to answer simple guest queries without human intervention, malfunctioning robotic dancers, and bellhop robots that got stuck on uneven surfaces. Ultimately, the hotel prioritized guest comfort over novelty, reintroducing human oversight in key service areas (CNET[5]). This case illustrates that full automation without ethical safeguards and human oversight can lead to operational inefficiencies rather than improvements.

As stated on the current hotel's website, Henn-na Hotel Tokyo Ginza, recognized by Guinness World Records as the world's first hotel staffed by robots, integrates cutting-edge technology to enhance guest experiences. The hotel combines humanoid robots, air purification robots, and floor-cleaning robots with modern amenities such as virtual reality (Meta Quest 2), Google Chromecast, and LG Styler garment care systems to provide a futuristic yet comfortable stay (Henn-na Hotel[6]).

In this chapter, we consider only the use of humanoid robots "employed" by the hotel. Upon arrival, guests are welcomed by front desk humanoid robots that assist with check-in. These multilingual robots communicate in English, Korean, Japanese, and Chinese, making the process seamless for international travelers (Skubis et al. 2024). Although the robots facilitate check-in and key distribution, human staff are also present to ensure a smooth experience. In addition to humanoid robots, the hotel utilizes air purification robots to maintain a clean environment and floor-cleaning robots for automated maintenance.

Beyond robotic assistance, the hotel offers innovative guest services. Each room is equipped with an LG Styler, allowing guests to steam-clean clothes, remove wrinkles, and freshen fabrics without the need for professional dry cleaning. Google Chromecast enables streaming entertainment on large screens, while virtual reality headsets (Meta Quest 2) can be rented for an immersive digital experience. Guests can also enjoy the hotel's lounge services, which provide complimentary breakfast, tea, and evening drinks, including a selection of Japanese craft beers available at an additional cost.

For guests seeking convenient transportation, the hotel offers LUUP electronic kickboard rentals. This service allows travelers to navigate the city with ease, though a Japanese license is required for operation. Additionally, the hotel provides practical amenities such as parcel delivery services (Yamato Transport), an automated external defibrillator (AED) for emergencies, an ice machine, vending machines, a coin-operated laundry, and a comic rental service.

While automation plays a central role in the hotel's operations, human staff remain integral to ensuring a smooth and enjoyable experience. The blend of robotic efficiency and human oversight makes Henn-na Hotel a pioneer in hospitality innovation, demonstrating how technology can enhance comfort and convenience without compromising guest satisfaction.

## 4.2 Humanoid Robots in Healthcare: Possibilities of Usage, Autonomy, Decision-Making, and Ethical Implications

Humanoid robots in healthcare enterprises have reshaped medical practices, patient care, and administrative processes. Humanoid robots such as Pepper, NAO, and Telenoid are increasingly used in diverse healthcare settings, including hospitals, eldercare facilities, and rehabilitation centers. These robots perform tasks ranging from patient interaction and assistance to complex data management, showcasing varying levels of autonomy and decision-making capabilities. They are designed to mimic human interaction, making them particularly effective in roles that require communication, empathy, and precision.

Their applications span patient care, rehabilitation, surgical assistance, and even administrative support, thereby addressing critical gaps in healthcare systems worldwide (Broadbent et al. 2018; Shishehgar et al. 2018). However, their implementation must align with ethical and regulatory requirements, particularly those outlined in the EU AI Act, which classifies healthcare AI applications as high-risk, requiring strict oversight, transparency, and accountability.

### *4.2.1 Patient Care and Monitoring*

One of the primary roles of humanoid (service) robots in healthcare is to enhance patient care through personalized interaction. Studies have shown that robots like Pepper can improve patient engagement, particularly in elderly care and dementia management, by providing cognitive stimulation, companionship, and emotional support (Moyle et al. 2014; Robinson et al. 2016). Additionally, robots assist in monitoring patient health by collecting vital signs and facilitating telemedicine consultations, thereby improving efficiency and reducing the workload on medical staff (Kachouie et al. 2014).

Despite these advantages, ethical concerns arise regarding the accuracy and privacy of patient data, the potential for over-reliance on robotic systems, and the need for explicit patient consent before AI-driven healthcare interventions are conducted. The GDPR mandates stringent data protection requirements, ensuring that patient information is securely handled and that AI-powered monitoring does not compromise patient autonomy.

From an ethical perspective, the deployment of humanoid robots in healthcare raises critical concerns regarding privacy, data security, informed consent, and human oversight. Ethical dilemmas also arise in the context of patient autonomy and the potential for over-reliance on robotic systems, which may impact the quality of human-centered care (Sharkey & Sharkey 2012; Vallor 2016). For instance, in elderly care facilities, while robots enhance social interaction and assist with routine tasks, they should not replace essential human care, as doing so may lead to emotional neglect and reduced socialization.

However, humanoid robots significantly enhance patient care by providing real-time health monitoring, medication management, and personalized interaction. Robots like Pepper and NAO are deployed in hospitals and eldercare facilities to monitor vital signs, remind patients to take their medication, and offer companionship to alleviate feelings of loneliness, particularly among elderly patients (Moyle et al. 2014; Robinson et al. 2016). These robots can collect data on heart rate, blood pressure, and oxygen levels, transmitting this information to healthcare professionals for timely intervention (Kachouie et al. 2014).

Decision-making autonomy in healthcare robots varies from fully autonomous diagnostic tools to semi-autonomous systems that support medical professionals. While AI-driven robots can analyze medical data and suggest treatment options, final decisions are typically reserved for human healthcare providers to ensure accountability and ethical integrity (Topol 2019). This collaborative model underlines the necessity of maintaining human oversight to mitigate risks associated with algorithmic biases and errors. As Solaiman and Malik (2025) indicate, the AI Act is intended to complement the GDPR but does not address its shortcomings. The GDPR faces issues such as under-resourced authorities, ineffective complaint mechanisms, and jurisdictional conflicts, which may also affect the AI Act's implementation. Notably, neither regulation grants patients the right to object to AI-driven decisions. While the AI Act allows individuals to request explanations about AI's role in decision-making, this falls short of providing a right to object—an omission that could have significant future implications (Solaiman & Malik 2025).

### 4.2.2 Telemedicine and Human–Robot Interaction (HRI): Ensuring Ethical AI Integration

In telemedicine, humanoid robots can act as intermediaries, facilitating virtual consultations between doctors and patients, so they can be perceived rather as virtual avatars. This capability is especially crucial in remote areas where access to healthcare services is limited. However, while telemedicine robots improve healthcare accessibility, their ability to make real-time patient assessments raises ethical concerns about liability and diagnostic accuracy. The AI Act emphasizes the need for explainable AI (XAI) principles, ensuring that any AI-driven diagnosis or recommendation is transparent and interpretable by healthcare providers and patients alike. The integration of humanoid robots in telehealth improves patient outcomes by ensuring continuous monitoring and immediate response to medical emergencies (Koceska et al. 2019; Tavakoli et al. 2020).

HRI in healthcare settings is essential for user acceptance and trust. Research indicates that patients and healthcare professionals are more likely to accept robots that demonstrate empathetic behavior, clear communication, and reliability (de Graaf & Allouch 2013; Mutlu & Forlizzi 2008).

Designing robots with user-friendly interfaces and incorporating feedback mechanisms are essential for fostering positive HRI and ensuring effective integration into healthcare workflows (Bartneck et al. 2009; Flandorfer 2012).

However, ethical concerns regarding the psychological effects of robotic caregiving persist, particularly for vulnerable patients such as children and the elderly. AI-driven robots must be carefully designed to provide support without fostering over-dependence or emotional attachment, which could compromise patient well-being.

### *4.2.3 Rehabilitation and Physical Therapy*

In rehabilitation, humanoid robots support both physical and cognitive therapies. Robots like Robear and robotic exoskeletons like HAL (Hybrid Assistive Limb), Lokomat, or ReWalk Robotics assist patients with mobility impairments, aiding in exercises that promote muscle strength and coordination (Fasola & Matarić 2013; Siciliano & Khatib 2016). Their ability to provide consistent, repetitive motion makes them ideal for physical therapy, where repetitive tasks are essential for recovery.

Moreover, humanoid robots are used in cognitive rehabilitation for patients with brain injuries and neurological disorders, including stroke survivors and individuals with dementia. They engage patients in interactive activities designed to improve memory, attention, and problem-solving skills (Corallo et al. 2022). Studies have demonstrated that such robotic interventions can enhance cognitive functions and contribute to better rehabilitation outcomes (Tapus et al. 2009). Nonetheless, these robots must comply with ethical guidelines on medical AI, ensuring that their interventions do not result in unintended psychological effects, such as frustration from failed interactions or reduced motivation for human-led therapies.

### 4.2.4 Surgical Assistance: Enhancing Precision while Ensuring Oversight

Robotic devices may also play an essential role in surgical procedures, offering high precision and stability that surpass human capabilities in certain contexts. Although not humanoid, robotic surgical assistants like the da Vinci Surgical System incorporate humanoid-like functionalities, such as articulated arms and advanced visualization tools, enabling minimally invasive surgeries with reduced recovery times and lower risks of complications (Herron et al. 2008; Lanfranco et al. 2004).

These robots assist surgeons by providing enhanced dexterity, steady control, and the ability to perform complex maneuvers with minimal physical strain. Furthermore, robotic systems are integrated with AI algorithms that support decision-making during surgeries, such as identifying critical anatomical structures and predicting potential complications (Hashimoto et al. 2018; Sgarbura & Vasilescu 2010). However, even in robotic-assisted surgeries, ultimate decision-making authority must remain with human surgeons to align with regulatory and ethical standards. The AI Act mandates that surgical robots fall under high-risk AI classifications, requiring rigorous validation, human supervision, and compliance with explainability standards (European Commission 2021b).

### 4.2.5 Administrative and Logistical Support

Beyond direct patient care, humanoid robots improve the efficiency of healthcare operations by handling administrative and logistical tasks. They can manage patient records, schedule appointments, and deliver medical supplies within hospital premises, reducing the workload of healthcare staff and minimizing the risk of human error (Riek 2017; Tanaka et al. 2012).

In pandemic situations, such as the COVID-19 crisis, robots have been deployed to perform disinfection tasks, distribute personal protective equipment, and even assist in triage processes, thereby limiting human exposure to infectious diseases and maintaining hospital efficiency (Liu et al. 2021; Yang & Chew 2020).

### *4.2.6 Healthcare Applications of Humanoid Robots: Ethical Considerations, Human–Robot Interaction, and User Acceptance*

While humanoid robots have the potential to make changes in healthcare, their deployment must align with ethical considerations, patient rights, and stringent regulatory frameworks. The widespread usage of humanoid robots in healthcare raises critical ethical issues related to patient privacy, data security, and the potential dehumanization of care. The Union's General Data Protection Regulation (GDPR) and the AI Act provide a regulatory framework to ensure data protection and ethical AI deployment (European Commission 2021b). These regulations emphasize the necessity of human oversight, particularly in decision-making processes involving patient health.

Ethical concerns also revolve around the potential loss of human touch in caregiving, as over-reliance on robots could diminish the quality of empathetic, person-centered care. Maintaining a balance between technological efficiency and human compassion is essential for ethical healthcare practices (Sharkey & Sharkey 2012; Vallor 2016).

Effective HRI is crucial for the successful integration of humanoid robots in healthcare. User acceptance depends on the robot's ability to demonstrate empathy, reliability, and clear communication. Designing robots with intuitive interfaces and incorporating feedback from both patients and healthcare professionals are key strategies to enhance HRI (de Graaf & Allouch 2013; Flandorfer 2012).

Studies have shown that cultural factors, patient age, and prior exposure to technology influence acceptance levels. Therefore, customization of robotic systems to meet the specific needs and preferences of diverse patient populations is vital for their widespread adoption (Broadbent et al. 2018; Mutlu & Forlizzi 2008).

Ozturkcan and Merdin-Uygur (2021) explore the role of humanoid service robots (HSRs) in healthcare, particularly during COVID-19. Their human-like design makes them ideal for hospitals, where they assist in patient monitoring, reducing human contact, and delivering medical supplies. Examples include Mitra in India, which connected COVID-19 patients with families, Tommy in Italy, which minimized frontline exposure, and SRs in Rwanda performing up to 50% of technical tasks (Ozturkcan and Merdin-Uygur 2021).

While social robots improve efficiency and reduce costs, their acceptance varies by culture and perceived usefulness (Coco et al. 2018; Davis 1989). Concerns include potential dehumanization, social isolation, and emotional attachment to robots (Veruggio et al. 2016). The study highlights the need for policies ensuring social robots enhance, rather than replace, human caregivers, positioning them as a key solution for workforce shortages and hospital efficiency (Ministry of Social Affairs and Health 2018).

Key takeaways include:

- AI-driven humanoid robots must enhance, not replace, human caregivers. Over-reliance on AI can lead to depersonalization of care, negatively impacting patient outcomes.
- Transparency and accountability are essential. The EU AI Act mandates that healthcare AI systems be auditable, interpretable, and subject to regulatory review.
- Data privacy must be safeguarded. Humanoid robots collecting patient data must comply with GDPR requirements, ensuring secure and ethical use of sensitive information.

- Bias mitigation strategies must be implemented. AI models used in humanoid healthcare robots should be carefully monitored to avoid discriminatory decision-making in patient care.

Ultimately, humanoid robots should serve as complementary tools rather than replacements for human professionals, aligning technological advancements with medical ethics and patient-centered healthcare practices.

### *4.2.6.1 Pepper Robot*

Developed by SoftBank Robotics, Pepper is a humanoid robot designed to interact with people through conversation and touch. The integration of humanoid robots like *Pepper* in the healthcare sector addresses multiple challenges, including an aging global population, declining fertility rates, and the mental health burden on healthcare workers. According to *United Robotics Group*[7] and *Aldebaran*,[8] healthcare robots contribute to improved patient care, increased efficiency, and cost reduction across medical facilities.

Key contributions of Pepper in healthcare include:

- Rehabilitation aid: Pepper supports physical and cognitive therapeutic activities, assisting patients in their recovery process. Its interactive capabilities help engage patients in exercises and therapy sessions, fostering better rehabilitation outcomes.
- Health education and adherence: By providing personalized health information and medication reminders, Pepper enhances treatment adherence, ensuring patients understand their medical conditions and prescribed regimens. This contributes to improved patient outcomes and reduced hospital readmissions.

- Emotional support and patient engagement: As a social robot, Pepper helps boost patient morale by offering companionship and emotional support. It interacts through speech, gestures, and expressions, alleviating feelings of loneliness, particularly among elderly and long-term care patients.
- Hospital supply management optimization: Healthcare robots, including Pepper, streamline hospital logistics by assisting in the delivery of supplies, thereby increasing operational efficiency and allowing medical professionals to focus on patient care.
- Visitor guidance and navigation assistance: Pepper functions as a wayfinding assistant in hospital facilities, helping visitors and patient families navigate complex healthcare environments. This reduces the workload of healthcare staff, enabling them to concentrate on more critical tasks.

By automating routine tasks, Pepper alleviates the administrative burden on medical staff, allowing them to dedicate more time to personalized patient care. This leads to improved job satisfaction, reduced burnout, and enhanced overall efficiency in hospital operations.

As stated on the Aldebaran website, SoftBank has officially ceased production of its humanoid robot, Pepper, citing an adequate stock supply rather than direct restructuring plans.

Initially introduced in 2014 by CEO Masayoshi Son, Pepper was envisioned as a groundbreaking personal robot that would transform HRI. However, its market performance fell short of expectations, with limited functionality and declining sales ultimately leading to the discontinuation of new production.

Production at a Foxconn factory in China has already been halted as the number of unsold units mounted, forcing SoftBank to shut down the manufacturing line. Reports indicate that monthly sales dropped to fewer than 100 units, and as of 2021, SoftBank holds fewer than 2,000 remaining Pepper robots in stock. One of the primary limitations hindering Pepper's adoption is its outdated technology, including aging batteries and an obsolete Android operating system that lacks the latest security updates. Despite halting production, SoftBank management insists that Pepper will continue in some form, potentially with a redesigned model in the future (ZDNet,[9] *Asia Financial*[10]).

### *4.2.6.2 NAO Robot*

The NAO humanoid robot, developed by the French company Aldebaran Robotics, which was acquired by SoftBank Group in 2015, and known for its advanced AI, speech recognition, and interactive capabilities, is primarily used in education to enhance learning experiences. It serves as a teaching assistant, language tutor, and STEM learning tool, promoting student engagement through interactive lessons, personalized learning, and social skill development. Additionally, NAO supports children with special needs by providing structured, engaging, and adaptive interactions tailored to their individual learning requirements.

Beyond education, NAO has also been explored in healthcare settings. It assists therapists in rehabilitation exercises, supports elderly patients with companionship and cognitive activities, and aids in speech therapy and social interaction training, particularly for individuals with autism, as stated on the Aldebaran website.[11] Its ability to provide interactive and engaging experiences makes it a valuable tool for improving patient care and well-being. While education remains its primary domain, NAO's adaptability allows it to contribute to various sectors, including healthcare, customer service, and entertainment.

Blavette et al. (2022) investigated the use of the NAO humanoid robot in geriatric facilities to promote COVID-19 precautionary measures among older adults, particularly those with neurocognitive disorders. The study involved 124 participants and used an interactive robot-mediated activity combining verbal and non-verbal communication to demonstrate key preventive measures. Results showed high acceptance and perceived usefulness, with participants engaging through imitation and eye contact.

Despite its success, challenges included limited gestures, speech recognition issues, and the need for human facilitation. While effective for many, healthcare professionals noted reduced impact on individuals with severe cognitive impairments. The study supports Nao's potential in health education, highlighting social robots as valuable tools for improving engagement, comprehension, and adherence to health guidelines in geriatric care.

### *4.2.6.3 GR-1*

As aging populations and labor shortages put increasing pressure on healthcare systems, robotics companies are developing humanoid solutions to assist with patient care. One such innovation is the GR-1 humanoid robot, developed by Shanghai-based Fourier Intelligence, which aims to support healthcare facilities by assisting in patient mobility, therapy, and companionship (*Euronews*[12])

Standing 1.65 m tall and weighing 55 kg, the GR-1 can walk, avoid obstacles, and perform basic tasks such as holding bottles and picking up objects. More advanced functionalities include carrying patients from beds to wheelchairs, acting as a therapy assistant, and providing companionship for elderly individuals living alone. The robot's self-balancing system allows it to perform various programmed movements, such as sitting, standing, and even jumping (*Fourier*[13]).

China's National Health Commission estimates that the number of people aged 60 and over will rise from 280 million to over 400 million by 2035, increasing demand for medical services amid workforce shortages. The GR-1 is being developed to help alleviate these challenges by assisting caregivers and patients in hospitals and rehabilitation centers. Fourier Intelligence CEO Zen Koh envisions GR-1 filling gaps in rehabilitation by providing autonomous robotic interaction to support physical therapy and patient assistance.

Currently in the research and development phase, Fourier Intelligence expects to have a working prototype within two to three years. The company has extensive experience in rehabilitation robotics and exoskeleton technology, and it aims to integrate GR-1 into healthcare settings where robotic assistance is already being utilized.

The GR-1 was showcased at the World AI Conference in Shanghai alongside Tesla's Optimus humanoid prototype and other AI-powered robots. Among them was the X20 quadrupedal robot, designed for hazardous tasks such as toxic gas detection and emergency rescue operations.

As the demand for robotics in healthcare grows, humanoid robots like GR-1 may play a critical role in assisting medical professionals, improving patient care, and addressing labor shortages in hospitals and elderly care facilities.

#### *4.2.6.4 Robear*

Robear, developed by the RIKEN-SRK Collaboration Center for Human-Interactive Robot Research and Sumitomo Riko Company Limited, is an experimental nursing-care robot designed to assist elderly patients. It can lift patients from beds into wheelchairs and help them stand, providing "powerful yet gentle care." As the successor to RIBA and RIBA-II, Robear is significantly lighter at 140 kg compared to its predecessor's 230 kg, improving maneuverability and efficiency.

Equipped with advanced actuator units featuring low gear ratios, Robear ensures smooth, precise movements while minimizing strain on patients. Its torque and Smart Rubber tactile sensors enhance safety by allowing gentle handling. Additionally, the robot's extendable legs provide stability when lifting patients and retract for easier navigation through tight spaces (*The Guardian*[14]).

With Japan's rapidly aging population and increasing caregiver workload—where lifting patients is a major cause of lower back pain—Robear aims to alleviate physical strain on healthcare workers and improve elderly care. Although the project was discontinued at RIKEN in March 2015, lead researcher Toshiharu Mukai, now at Meijo University, continues to explore practical robotic solutions for caregiving. As robotic technology advances, Japan remains at the forefront of integrating humanoid and assistive robots into healthcare and other service industries (RIKEN[15]).

## 4.3 Humanoid Robots in Corporate Environments

Humanoid robots are increasingly being integrated into corporate environments, serving roles that range from digital assistants to customer service agents and even managerial positions. While these AI-driven humanoids improve efficiency and optimize decision-making processes, their presence in corporate structures raises ethical, psychological, and strategic challenges that must be addressed.

### *4.3.1 Humanoid Service Robots (HSRs) in Consumer-Facing and Workplace Roles*

The research by Mende et al. (2019) explores the psychological and behavioral effects of HSRs in corporate and consumer-facing environments. It examines the influence of HSRs on customer experiences, revealing that while these robots offer operational efficiencies, they also trigger psychological and behavioral responses in consumers.

The study highlights that HSRs can elicit discomfort due to their human-like appearance, leading to compensatory behaviors such as increased status consumption, social affiliation, and caloric intake. These reactions align with the "uncanny valley" effect, where consumers experience unease when faced with highly anthropomorphic robots (Mori et al. 2012). The research further identifies moderating factors, including social belongingness, perceived healthfulness of food, and the degree of mechanization in robot design. Findings suggest that HSRs are more effective when presented in environments that foster social interaction, and that reducing their human-like traits can mitigate consumer discomfort.

From a managerial perspective, companies integrating HSRs should track consumer responses and segment customers based on their affinity for technology. Providing consumers with the option to interact with either a human or a robot can improve satisfaction and reduce unintended consequences such as overspending or increased consumption (Mende et al. 2019). Additionally, the study suggests that HSRs may be particularly effective in high-status product sales and in environments where social engagement enhances consumer comfort. However, their presence in certain settings, such as all-you-can-eat restaurants, could lead to undesirable behaviors, such as excessive consumption. Future research should examine long-term consumer responses to HSRs, refine robot design features to minimize discomfort, and explore the broader implications of HRI in service industries.

### 4.3.2 Digital Assistants and Workplace Automation

In office settings, humanoid robots serve as digital assistants, streamlining administrative processes and optimizing workplace productivity. AI-driven humanoids facilitate scheduling, manage data analysis, and assist in decision-making by processing vast amounts of information in real time. These robots enhance human performance by providing data-driven insights, reducing repetitive tasks, and enabling employees to focus on complex problem-solving and creative tasks (Daugherty & Wilson 2018).

For example, humanoid robots integrated with natural language processing (NLP) technologies can interact with employees, answer queries, and automate routine administrative duties. Virtual assistants such as IBM Watson, Amelia, or Nadine are already employed in corporate environments to facilitate human–robot collaboration, demonstrating the practical benefits of AI-driven humanoid solutions in business operations.

### *4.3.2.1 Amelia*

Amelia is an AI system developed by the American software company IPsoft over 15 years. She is a virtual humanoid robot. Designed to perform various enterprise tasks as efficiently as human employees, Amelia integrates multiple AI technologies, including machine learning, natural language processing, document analysis, and automated reasoning.

Tested in several Fortune 1000 companies, Amelia rapidly processes instructional manuals to perform assigned tasks. Unlike simple word-for-word comprehension, the system contextualizes text and understands its overall meaning. Additionally, Amelia learns by observing her human and AI colleagues, improving over time.

Initially, Amelia had limited success in IT support, responding to customer queries with minimal accuracy. However, within one month, she successfully resolved 42% of common issues, and by the second month, her accuracy increased to 64%, demonstrating continuous learning and performance improvement (*Usine Digitale*[6]).

#### 4.3.2.2 Nadine

Nadine is one of the most realistic female humanoid social robots, modeled after Prof. Nadia Magnenat Thalman. Designed with a lifelike human appearance, including natural skin, hair, and highly realistic hands, Nadine exhibits socially intelligent behavior. She greets people, makes eye contact, and remembers past conversations. With the ability to communicate in multiple languages, she expresses emotions through facial expressions and gestures based on user interactions. Nadine can recognize individuals she has met before, recall personal details, and engage in meaningful, flowing conversations (MIRALab[17]).

Research on Nadine, a humanoid social robot, highlights the potential for robots to function effectively in workplace settings, particularly in customer service roles. In a study conducted at an insurance company, Nadine was evaluated based on customer interactions using survey questionnaires and aspect-based sentiment analysis. The findings indicate that while customers generally responded positively to Nadine's presence, functionality, and social etiquette, there were limitations related to response accuracy and expectations set by her human-like appearance. The study underlines the importance of balancing AI capabilities with realistic job expectations, as humanoid robots may struggle with complex, open-ended tasks due to constraints in data accessibility and conversational adaptability (Mishra et al. 2019).

Nadine can also be used in healthcare. She is designed to assist individuals with special needs, providing companionship, reading stories, showing images, facilitating video calls, sending emails, and maintaining communication with family members. As a human-assistive technology, Nadine aims to address the growing need for social care by acting as a personal coach or companion when human caregivers are unavailable (MIRALaB).

## 4.4 Humanoid Robots in Leadership and Management

Robots in supervisory roles elicit mixed reactions, inspiring both admiration and concern over job displacement. Research by Yam et al. (2022) highlights the advantages of robot supervisors, particularly their superior data-processing capabilities, which enable efficient data-driven decision-making. Studies by Gombolay et al. (2015) demonstrate that robots can outperform humans in task allocation and improve team coordination efficiency, leading to higher productivity in mixed human-robot teams. Additionally, granting robots authority over team coordination increases their perceived value. However, concerns persist regarding human trust, resistance to robotic authority, and potential job displacement.

Haesevoets et al. (2021) found that managers generally accept collaboration with machines, provided humans maintain a significant role in decision-making. AI in management is currently limited to routine decisions, but its full potential lies in strategic decision-making support, such as in mergers and acquisitions. The rise of humanoid robots in managerial roles is also examined through the lens of Responsible Leadership (RL), which prioritizes ethical and forward-thinking decision-making (Maak & Pless 2006; Skubis et al. 2023). Responsible leadership, as defined by Treviño et al. (2000), fosters ethical behavior and enhances organizational commitment and innovation. Humanoid robot CEOs, free from human biases and emotions, could consistently uphold ethical standards, reinforcing ethical and socially responsible workplace behavior in alignment with Treviño et al.'s (2000) leadership model.

### *4.4.1 Tang Yu: Virtual Humanoid CEO of NetDragon Websoft*

In August 2022, *NetDragon Websoft*, a Chinese gaming and digital education company, appointed Tang Yu, an AI-powered virtual humanoid robot, as the CEO of its subsidiary, *Fujian NetDragon Websoft*. This unprecedented move marked the introduction of a virtual executive into a real corporate leadership position, signaling a radical shift in the potential of AI within organizational management.

Tang Yu is designed to operate around the clock, serving as a real-time data processing hub and analytical engine for high-level decision-making. Her responsibilities encompass a wide range of executive tasks, including optimizing workflow efficiency, enhancing work quality, accelerating execution speed, and promoting logical, data-driven corporate strategy implementation (ShowMeTech 2023). Notably, she also contributes to risk management, talent development, and the cultivation of a fair workplace environment.

NetDragon emphasized that Tang Yu's leadership is central to their "AI + management" strategy and part of a broader vision to become a Metaverse organization. Tang Yu's operational model integrates big data analytics, machine learning, and real-time feedback loops, allowing her to make strategic decisions with speed and precision. Within six months of her appointment, the company's stock value reportedly increased by up to 10%, outperforming the Hang Seng Index (ShowMeTech 2023), reinforcing the argument that AI can deliver concrete business benefits in executive roles.

Despite her efficiency, Tang Yu remains a non-sentient algorithmic system. She lacks emotional intelligence, ethical intuition, and subjective judgment. Thus, her actions are always under human supervision, ensuring alignment with corporate goals, compliance with legal frameworks, and the ability to intervene in unexpected scenarios. These concerns are particularly aligned with European Union AI policy, which mandates human oversight, especially in high-risk applications such as decision-making in corporate governance (European Commission 2020; European Parliament 2019).

Tang Yu symbolizes a new archetype of leadership—data-centric, impartial, tireless, and programmable, challenging traditional notions of authority and executive agency in corporate structures.

### *4.4.2 Mika: Humanoid Robot CEO of Dictador*

Around the same time in 2022, *Dictador*, a luxury rum producer based in Poland, appointed Mika, a physical humanoid robot, as its CEO. Unlike Tang Yu, who exists in virtual form, Mika is a real-life humanoid robot whose physical presence and aesthetic are essential to her executive identity and brand strategy.

Mika was developed not just to manage internal operations but also to serve as the public face of Dictador and act as a board member responsible for overseeing the company's innovative *Arthouse Spirits DAO* (Decentralized Autonomous Organization) project. Her primary tasks include interacting with the DAO community, managing a treasury of rare rums worth over $50 million, and curating communications and experiences for the luxury clientele (Skubis & Wodarski 2023). She facilitates direct engagement with members, offers unique social interaction opportunities, and embodies Dictador's vision of blending heritage with futurism.

Mika represents a fusion of AI, robotics, and Web3, targeting a digitally native, trendsetting audience. Her appointment also aligns with Dictador's ambition to push the boundaries of luxury branding, marketing, and community management. While she has been praised for her precision, reliability, and efficiency, Mika's core strengths lie in strategic brand positioning and personalized communication—roles that are increasingly significant in consumer-oriented industries.

Despite her prominence, Mika does not operate independently. Strategic decisions, especially those involving financial risk or ethical consequences, are still reviewed and authorized by human executives. Her presence is intended to augment human leadership, not replace it, and her actions remain embedded within a framework of human oversight and corporate responsibility.

Mika illustrates a different trajectory of AI in leadership—personified, emotive in design, and focused on human-facing roles, offering a glimpse into how AI can support experiential branding and community-led governance in luxury markets.

## Notes

1 https://www.hansonrobotics.com/sophia/.
2 https://uk.newsroom.ibm.com/2016-Mar-09-Hilton-and-IBM-Pilot-Connie-The-Worlds-First-Watson-Enabled-Hotel-Concierge - accessed on 13.02.2025.
3 https://eu.usatoday.com/story/travel/roadwarriorvoices/2016/03/09/introducing-connie-hiltons-new-robot-concierge/81525924/ - accessed on 13.02.2025.
4 https://www.robotlab.com/pepper-robot-for-hospitality?srsltid=AfmBOool7EblcNtSAf5bv0SVsTOpfKjHZ26vp4XbG_4KWMNLBAx_P8l5 – 13.02.2025.
5 https://www.cnet.com/culture/hotel-in-japan-fires-half-its-robot-staff-for-being-bad-at-their-jobs/.
6 https://tokyo-ginza.hennnahotel.com/our-hotel/.
7 https://unitedrobotics.group/en-us/industries/healthcare - accessed on 11.02.2025.
8 https://aldebaran.com/pepper/# - accessed on 11.02.2025.
9 https://www.zdnet.com/article/softbank-halted-pepper-production-as-it-has-enough-stock-rather-than-for-restructuring-reasons/ - accessed on 11.02.2025.
10 https://www.asiafinancial.com/softbank-claims-pepper-the-robot-still-alive-despite-sales-dive - accessed on 11.02.2025.
11 https://aldebaran.com/nao-activities-2/ - 11.02.2025.
12 https://www.euronews.com/next/2023/07/12/worlds-first-mass-produced-humanoid-robot-to-tackle-labour-shortages-amid-ageing-populatio - accessed on 11.02.2025.

13 https://www.fftai.com/products-gr1 - accessed on 11.02.2025.
14 https://www.theguardian.com/technology/2015/feb/27/robear-bear-shaped-nursing-care-robot - 12.02.2025.
15 https://www.riken.jp/en/news_pubs/research_news/pr/2015/20150223_2/ - accessed on 12.02.2025.
16 https://www.usine-digitale.fr/article/voici-amelia-l-intelligence-artificielle-capable-d-apprendre-des-erreurs-de-ses-collegues.N288394 - accessed on 20.02.2025.
17 https://www.miralab.ch/index.php/nadine-social-robot/ - accessed on 20.02.2025.

## References


AI Act. (2024). European Parliament legislative resolution of 13 March 2024 on the proposal for a regulation of the European Parliament and of the Council on laying down harmonised rules on Artificial Intelligence (Artificial Intelligence Act) and amending certain Union Legislative Acts (COM(2021)0206–C9-0146/2021–2021/0106(COD)).

Bartneck, C., Kulić, D., Croft, E., & Zoghbi, S. (2009). Measurement instruments for the anthropomorphism, animacy, likeability, perceived intelligence, and perceived safety of robots. *International Journal of Social Robotics*, 1(1), 71–81. https://doi.org/10.1007/s12369-008-0001-3

Belanche, D., Casaló, L. V., Flavián, C., & Schepers, J. (2019). Service robot implementation: A theoretical framework and research agenda. *The Service Industries Journal*, 40(3–4), 203–225. https://doi.org/10.1080/02642069.2019.1672666

Blavette, L., Rigaud, A. S., Anzalone, S. M., Kergueris, C., Isabet, B., Dacunha, S., & Pino, M. (2022). A robot-mediated activity using the Nao robot to promote COVID-19 precautionary measures among older adults in geriatric facilities. *International Journal of Environmental Research and Public Health*, 19(9), 5222. https://doi.org/10.3390/ijerph19095222

Bowen, J., & Morosan, C. (2018). Beware hospitality industry: The robots are coming. *Worldwide Hospitality and Tourism Themes*, 10(6), 726–733.

Breazeal, C. (2003). Toward sociable robots. *Robotics and Autonomous Systems*, 42, 167–175.

Broadbent, E., Garrett, J., Jepsen, N., Li Ogilvie, V., Ahn, H. S., Robinson, H., Peri, K., Kerse, N., Rouse, P., Pillai, A., & MacDonald, B. (2018). Using robots at home to support patients with chronic obstructive pulmonary disease: Pilot randomized controlled trial. *Journal of Medical Internet Research*. https://doi.org/10.2196/jmir.8640

Brynjolfsson, E., & McAfee, A. (2014). *The second machine age: Work, progress, and prosperity in a time of brilliant technologies*. New York, NY: W. W. Norton & Company.

Choi, S., Liu, S. Q., & Mattila, A. S. (2019). "How may i help you?" says a robot: Examining language styles in the service encounter. *International Journal of Hospitality Management*, 82, 32–38. https://doi.org/10.1016/j.ijhm.2019.03.026

Coco, K., Kangasniemi, M., & Rantanen, T. (2018). Care personnel's attitudes and fears toward care robots in elderly care: A comparison of data from the care personnel in Finland and Japan. *Journal of Nursing Scholarship*, 50, 634–644.

Coeckelbergh, M. (2021). How to use virtue ethics for thinking about the moral standing of social robots: A relational interpretation in terms of practices, habits, and performance. *International Journal of Social Robotics*, 13, 31–40. https://doi.org/10.1007/s12369-020-00707-z

Corallo, F., Maresca, G., Formica, C., Bonanno, L., Bramanti, A., Parasporo, N., Giambò, F. M., De Cola, M. C., & Lo Buono, V. (2022). Humanoid robot use in cognitive rehabilitation of patients with severe brain injury: A pilot study. *Journal of Clinical Medicine*, 11(10), 2940. https://doi.org/10.3390/jcm11102940

Daugherty, P. R., & Wilson, H. J. (2018). *Human + machine: Reimagining work in the age of AI*. Boston, MA: Harvard Business Review Press.

Davis, F. D. (1989) Perceived usefulness, perceived ease of use, and user acceptance of information technology. *MIS Quarterly*, 13(3), 319–340.

de Graaf, M. M. A., & Allouch, S. B. (2013). Exploring influencing variables for the acceptance of social robots. *Robotics and Autonomous Systems*, 61(12), 1476–1486. https://doi.org/10.1016/j.robot.2013.07.007

European Commission. (2019). *Directorate-general for communications networks, content and technology*. European Commission.

European Commission. (2020). White paper on artificial intelligence: A European approach to excellence and trust. https://commission.europa.eu/publications/white-paper-artificial-intelligence-european-approach-excellence-and-trust_en#details

European Commission. (2021a). *Coordinated plan on artificial intelligence*. European Commission.

European Commission. (2021b). Proposal for a regulation on a European approach for artificial intelligence (artificial intelligence act). https://eur-lex.europa.eu/legal-content/EN/TXT/?uri=CELEX%3A52021PC0206

European Parliament. (2019). European Parliament resolution of 12 February 2019 on a comprehensive European industrial policy on artificial intelligence and robotics. https://www.europarl.europa.eu/doceo/document/TA-8-2019-0081_EN.html

Fasola, J., & Matarić, M. J. (2013). A socially assistive robot exercise coach for the elderly. *Journal of Human-Robot Interaction*, 2(2), 3–32.

Flandorfer, P. (2012). Population ageing and socially assistive robots for elderly persons: The importance of sociodemographic factors for user acceptance. *International Journal of Population Research*. https://doi.org/10.1155/2012/829835

Floridi, L., & Cowls, J. (2019). A unified framework of five principles for AI in society. *Harvard Data Science Review*, 1(1). https://doi.org/10.1162/99608f92.8cd550d1

Fong, T., Nourbakhsh, I., & Dautenhahn, K. (2003). A survey of socially interactive robots. *Robotics and Autonomous Systems*, 42(3–4), 143–166.

Gombolay, M. C., Gutierrez, R. A., Clarke, S. G., Sturla, G. F., & Shah, J. A. (2015). Decision- making authority, team efficiency and human worker satisfaction in mixed human–robot teams. *Autonomous Robots*, 39(3), 293–312. https://doi.org/10.1007/s10514-015-9457-9

Haesevoets, T., De Cremer, D., Dierckx, K., & Van Hiel, A. (2021). Human-machine collaboration in managerial decision making. *Computers in Human Behavior*, 119. https://doi.org/10.1016/j.chb.2021.106730

Hashimoto, D. A., Rosman, G., Rus, D., & Meireles, O. R. (2018). Artificial intelligence in surgery: Promises and perils. *Annals of Surgery*, 268(1), 70–76. https://doi.org/10.1097/SLA.0000000000002693

Herron, D. M., Marohn, M., & The SAGES-MIRA Robotic Surgery Consensus Group. (2008). A consensus document on robotic surgery. *Surgical Endoscopy*, 22, 313–325. https://doi.org/10.1007/s00464-007-9727-5

Huang, M.-H., & Rust, R. T. (2018). Artificial intelligence in service. *Journal of Service Research*, 21(2), 155–172. https://doi.org/10.1177/1094670517752459

Ivanov, S., Seyitoğlu, F., & Markova, M. (2020). Hotel managers' perceptions towards the use of robots: A mixed-methods approach. *Information Technology & Tourism*, 22(4), 505–535. https://doi.org/10.1007/s40558-020-00187-x

Ivanov, S., & Webster, C. (2019). *Robots, artificial intelligence, and service automation in travel, tourism, and hospitality*. Bingley: Emerald Publishing.

Kachouie, R., Sedighadeli, S., Khosla, R., & Chu, M. T. (2014). Socially assistive robots in elderly care: A mixed-method systematic literature review. *International Journal of Human-Computer Interaction*, 30(5), 369–393. https://doi.org/10.1080/10447318.2013.873278

Kaplan, J. (2016). *Artificial intelligence: What everyone needs to know*. Oxford: Oxford University Press.

Koceska, N., Koceski, S., Beomonte Zobel, P., Trajkovik, V., & Garcia, N. (2019). A telemedicine robot system for assisted and independent living. *Sensors*, 19(4), 834. https://doi.org/10.3390/s19040834

Lanfranco, A. R., Castellanos, A. E., Desai, J. P., & Meyers, W. C. (2004). Robotic surgery: A current perspective. *Annals of Surgery*, 239(1), 14–21. https://doi.org/10.1097/01.sla.0000103020.19595.7d

Liu, L., Liu, Y., & Gao, X.-Z. (2021). Impacts of human robot proxemics on human concentration-training games with humanoid robots. *Healthcare*, 9(7), 894. https://doi.org/10.3390/healthcare9070894

Lu, L., Cai, R., & Gursoy, D. (2019). Developing and validating a service robot integration willingness scale. *International Journal of Hospitality Management*, 80, 36–51.

Maak, T., & Pless, N. M. (2006). Responsible leadership in a stakeholder society – A relational perspective. *Journal of Business Ethics*, 66(1), 99–115.

Mende, M., Scott, M. L., van Doorn, J., Grewal, D., & Shanks, I. (2019). Service robots rising. *Journal of Marketing Research*, 56(4), 535–549. https://doi.org/10.1177/0022243718822827

Ministry of Social Affairs and Health. (2018). *The well-being and health sector's artificial intelligence and robotics programme*. Helsinki: Ministry of Social Affairs and Health.

Mishra, N., Ramanathan, M., Satapathy, R., Cambria, E., & Magnenat-Thalmann, N. (2019). Can a humanoid robot be part of the organizational workforce? A user study leveraging sentiment analysis. *2019 28th IEEE International Conference on Robot and Human Interactive Communication (RO-MAN)*, 1–6. IEEE. https://doi.org/10.1109/RO-MAN46459.2019.8956349

Mori, M., MacDorman, K. F., & Kageki, N. (2012). The uncanny valley. *IEEE Robotics and Automation Magazine*, 19(2), 98–100. https://doi.org/10.1109/MRA.2012.2192811

Moyle, W., Jones, C., Cooke, M., O'Dwyer, S., Sung, B., & Drummond, S. (2014). Connecting the person with dementia and family: A feasibility study of a telepresence robot. *BMC Geriatrics*. https://doi.org/10.1186/1471-2318-14-7

Murphy, J., Gretzel, U., & Pesonen, J. (2019). Marketing robot services in hospitality and tourism: the role of anthropomorphism. *Journal of Travel & Tourism Marketing*, 36(7), 784–795. https://doi.org/10.1080/10548408.2019.1571983

Mutlu, B., & Forlizzi, J. (2008). Robots in organizations: The role of workflow, social, and environmental factors in human-robot interaction. *3rd ACM/IEEE International Conference on Human-Robot Interaction (HRI)*, Amsterdam, Netherlands, 287–294. https://doi.org/10.1145/1349822.1349860

Noreils, F. R. (2024). Humanoid robots at work: Where are we? arXiv. https://doi.org/10.48550/arXiv.2404.04249

Ozturkcan, S., & Merdin-Uygur, E. (2021). Humanoid service robots: The future of healthcare? *Journal of Information Technology Teaching Cases*, 12(2), 163–169. https://doi.org/10.1177/20438869211003905

Palrão, T., Rodrigues, R. I., Madeira, A., Mendes, A. S., & Lopes, S. (2023). Robots in tourism and hospitality: The perception of future professionals. *Human Behavior and Emerging Technologies*, 2023, 7172152. https://doi.org/10.1155/2023/7172152

Parasuraman, A., Zeithaml, V. A., & Berry, L. L. (1988). SERVQUAL: A multiple-item scale for measuring consumer perceptions of service quality. *Journal of Retailing*, 64(1), 12–40.

Qiu, H., Li, M., Shu, B., & Bai, B. (2020). Enhancing hospitality experience with service robots: The mediating role of rapport building. *Journal of Hospitality Marketing & Management*, 29(3), 247–268.

Riek, L. D. (2017). Healthcare robotics. *Communication ACM*, 60(11), 68–78. https://doi.org/10.1145/3127874

Robinson, H., Broadbent, E., & MacDonald, B. (2016). Group sessions with Paro in a nursing home: Structure, observations and interviews. *Australasian Journal on Ageing*, 35(2), 106–112. https://doi.org/10.1111/ajag.12199

Rosete, A., Soares, B., Salvadorinho, J., Reis, J., & Amorim, M. (2020). *Service robots in the hospitality industry: An exploratory literature review*. Springer.

Seyitoğlu, F., & Ivanov, S. (2020). Service robots as a tool for physical distancing in tourism. *Current Issues in Tourism*, 24(12), 1631–1634. https://doi.org/10.1080/13683500.2020.1774518

Sgarbura, O., & Vasilescu, C. (2010). The decisive role of the patient-side surgeon in robotic surgery. *Surgical Endoscopy*, 24, 3149–3155 (2010). https://doi.org/10.1007/s00464-010-1108-9

Sharkey, A., & Sharkey, N. (2012). Granny and the robots: ethical issues in robot care for the elderly. *Ethics and Information Technology*, 14, 27–40. https://doi.org/10.1007/s10676-010-9234-6

Sharkey, A., & Sharkey, N. (2020). We need to talk about deception in social robotics! *Ethics and Information Technology*, 23(3), 309–316. https://doi.org/10.1007/s10676-020-09573-9

Shishehgar, M., Kerr, D., & Blake, J. (2018). A systematic review of research into how robotic technology can help older people. *Smart Health*, 7–8, 1–18. https://doi.org/10.1016/j.smhl.2018.03.002

ShowMeTech. (2023). Meet 'Tang Yu', the first AI CEO of a company. Retrieved from: https://www.showmetech.com.br/en/tang-yu-a-primeira-aiceo-em-uma-empresa/

Siciliano, B., & Khatib, O. (Eds.). (2016). *Springer handbook of robotics* (2nd ed.). Heidelberg: Springer.

Skubis, I. (2024). The EU guidelines on roboethics and ethics of sex robots. In: Lütge, C., Kriebitz, A., Max, R., & Corrigan, C., *The Elgar companion to applied AI ethics*. Edward Elgar Publishing, 397–409.

Skubis, I. (2024a). *Ética, terminología, opiniones y el mercado de SexTech: un análisis multidisciplinario sobre los robots sexuales*. Wydawnictwo Politechniki Śląskiej. ISBN: 978-83-7880-957-9

Skubis, I. (2024b). Seksroboty – Zarządzanie Etyką i Zarządzanie Innowacjami w Branży Sextech. *Management and Quality*, 6(3), 211–232.

Skubis, I. (2025). Exploring the potential and perceptions of social robots in tourism and hospitality: Insights from industry executives and technology evaluation. *International Journal of Social Robotics*, 17, 59–72. https://doi.org/10.1007/s12369-024-01197-z

Skubis, I., Akahome, J., & Bijańska, J. (2023). *The brain drain syndrome and the role of responsible leadership in health care service organisation in Nigeria.* Scientific Papers of Silesian University of Technology – Organization and Management Series, vol. 176, 599–615. https://doi.org/10.29119/1641-3466.2023.176.34

Skubis, I., Mesjasz-Lech, A., & Nowakowska-Grunt, J. (2024). Humanoid robots in tourism and hospitality – Exploring managerial, ethical, and societal challenges. *Applied Sciences*, 14(24), 11823. https://doi.org/10.3390/app142411823

Skubis, I., & Mosek, M., (2025). Human-like and humanoid virtual influencers (HVIs): Transforming digital marketing and consumer engagement. *Linguistic and Philosophical Investigations*, 24(1), 170–190.

Skubis, I., & Wodarski, K. (2023). Humanoid robots in managerial positions – Decision-making process and human oversight. *Scientific Papers of Silesian University of Technology*, 189, 573–596. https://doi.org/10.29119/1641-3466.2023.189.36

Skubis, I., Wolniak, R., & Grebski, W. W. (2024). AI and human-centric approach in smart cities management: Case studies from Silesian and lesser Poland voivodships. *Sustainability*, 16, 8279. https://doi.org/10.3390/su16188279

Solaiman, B., & Malik, A. (2025). Regulating algorithmic care in the European Union: Evolving doctor–patient models through the Artificial Intelligence Act (AI-Act) and the liability directives. *Medical Law Review*, 33(1), fwae033. https://doi.org/10.1093/medlaw/fwae033

Sostero, M. (2020). *Automation and robots in services: review of data and taxonomys.* Seville: European Commission, JRC121893.

Tanaka, M., Ishii, A., Yamano, E., Ogikubo, H., Okazaki, M., Kamimura, K., Konishi, Y., Emoto, S., & Watanabe, Y. (2012). Effect of a human-type communication robot on cognitive function in elderly women living alone. *Medical Science Monitor*, 18(9), CR550–CR557. https://doi.org/10.12659/msm.883350

Tapus, A., Tapus, C., & Matarić, M. J. (2009). The use of socially assistive robots in the design of intelligent cognitive therapies for people with dementia. In *2009 IEEE International Conference on Rehabilitation Robotics (ICORR)*. IEEE. https://doi.org/10.1109/ICORR.2009.5209501

Tavakoli, M., Carriere, J., & Torabi, N. (2020). Robotics, smart wearable technologies, and autonomous intelligent systems for healthcare during the COVID-19 pandemic: An analysis of the state of the art and future vision. *Advanced Intelligent Systems*, 2(7), 2000071.

Topol, E. (2019). *Deep medicine: How artificial intelligence can make healthcare human again*. New York: Basic Books.

Treviño, L. K., Hartman, L. P., & Brown, M. (2000). Moral person and moral manager: Her executives develop a reputation for ethic leadership. *California Management Review*, 42, 128–142. https://doi.org/10.2307/41166057.

Tuomi, A., Tussyadiah, I. P., & Stienmetz, J. (2020). Applications and implications of service robots in hospitality. *Cornell Hospitality Quarterly*, 61(4), 428–444.

Tussyadiah, I., & Park, S. (2018). Consumer evaluation of hotel service robots. In *Information and communication technologies in tourism*. https://doi.org/10.1007/978-3-319-72923-7_24

Tussyadiah, I. A. (2020). Review of research into automation in tourism: launching the annals of tourism research curated collection on artificial intelligence and robotics in tourism. *Annals of Tourism Research*, 81, 102883.

Vallor, S. (2016). *Technology and the virtues: A philosophical guide to a future worth wanting*. Oxford: Oxford University Press.

Vanderelst, D., & Winfield, A. (2018). An architecture for ethical robots inspired by the simulation theory of cognition. *Cognitive Systems Research*, 48, 56–66. https://doi.org/10.1016/j.cogsys.2017.04.002

Venkatesh, V., Morris, M. G., Davis, G. B., & Davis, F. D. (2003). User acceptance of information technology: Toward a unified view. *MIS Quarterly*, 27(3), 425–478. https://doi.org/10.2307/30036540

Venkatesh, V., Thong, J. Y. L., & Xu, X. (2016). Unified theory of acceptance and use of technology: A synthesis and the road ahead. *Journal of the Association for Information Systems*, 17(5). https://doi.org/10.17705/1jais.00428

Veruggio, G., Operto, F., & Bekey, G. (2016). Roboethics: Social and ethical implications of robotics. In: Siciliano B & Khatib O (eds.), *Springer handbook of robotics*. Berlin: Springer International Publishing, 1499–1524.

Vollmer, A. L., Read, R., Trippas, D., & Belpaeme, T. (2018). Children conform, adults resist: A robot group induced peer pressure on normative social conformity. *Science Robotics*, 3(21), eaat7111. https://doi.org/10.1126/scirobotics.aat7111

Wirtz, J., Patterson, P. G., Kunz, W. H., Gruber, T., Lu, V. N., Paluch, S., & Martins, A. (2018). Brave new world: Service robots in the frontline. *Journal of Service Management*, 29(5), 907–931. https://doi.org/10.1108/JOSM-04-2018-0119

Yam, K. C., Goh, E.-Y., Fehr, R., Lee, R., Soh, H., & Gray, K. (2022). When your boss is a robot: Workers are more spiteful to robot supervisors that seem more human. *Journal of Experimental Social Psychology*, 102, 1–12. https://doi.org/10.1016/j.jesp.2022.104360

Yang, J., & Chew, E. (2020). A systematic review for service humanoid robotics model in hospitality. *International Journal of Social Robotics*, 13, 1397–1410. https://doi.org/10.1007/s12369-020-00724-y

# Chapter 5

# Conclusion

We live in a time when technology is reshaping the way we work, connect, and do business, faster than ever before. At the same time, people's expectations of companies are changing, and the world of business is becoming increasingly complex and competitive. In this context, traditional ways of managing organizations are no longer enough. Businesses must rethink how they operate, make decisions, and create value, not just with new tools, but with new mindsets.

This book, *Innovative Business Strategies*, sets out to explore these changes and challenges. Through its four chapters, it looks closely at how innovation, sustainability, financial strategy, and emerging technologies, especially humanoid robots, are influencing the way organizations function today. What emerged is a clear message: To thrive in the digital world, companies need to be flexible, forward-thinking, and, above all, human-centered.

As the digital economy continues to unfold, it is not just about keeping up with the latest trends or adopting the newest technologies. It is about understanding what these changes mean for people, inside and outside the organization, and ensuring that progress serves not only performance, but also purpose and responsibility. Whether it is adopting

DOI: 10.1201/9781003739364-5

innovative management models, building sustainable strategies, rethinking financial decisions, or welcoming robots into the workplace, success today depends on a thoughtful, balanced approach that puts people and ethics at the center of transformation.

It seems that the most appropriate form to conclude the above considerations, which have been carried out in four chapters of this work, is to summarize them.

The first chapter focuses on the importance of innovative management models in the context of digital transformation and a dynamically changing business environment. It points out that the integration of modern technologies and flexible organizational strategies is key to achieving competitiveness and efficiency in business operations. In an era of globalization, rising customer expectations, and rapid technological advances, organizations must constantly adapt their structures, processes, and strategies to meet new challenges and seize opportunities. It emphasizes that innovative management models allow companies to optimize operations, improve operational efficiency, and increase the value delivered to customers.

The use of modern tools such as artificial intelligence, big data, digital platforms, and VR and AR technology enables companies not only to automate processes but also to make more accurate business decisions based on data analysis. Management innovations contribute to the competitiveness of companies by increasing operational flexibility, better managing resources, and implementing strategies that are adapted to dynamic market changes. Organizations that are able to operate effectively in the digital environment gain a competitive advantage through innovative approaches to managing relationships with customers, suppliers, and business partners. Challenges to implementing innovation, such as high investment costs, resistance to change, and technological risks, were also pointed out. Management innovation is becoming the foundation for success in the digital economy, and organizations that effectively implement modern solutions are more likely to grow rapidly and achieve strategic business goals.

The second chapter is devoted to the analysis of sustainable innovations, which, although still at an early stage of research compared to traditional innovations, play a key role in reducing pollution, saving energy, and promoting green development. Sustainable innovation can reduce environmental pollution, save energy, and promote sustainable green development in which environmental protection and enterprise competitiveness are aligned.

With the increasing importance of sustainability in innovation activities, both researchers and practitioners are focusing on understanding how to align sustainability goals with innovation practices. As a result, a growing body of literature points to three key perspectives: Internal management, external relationships, and performance evaluation.

The literature review suggests that sustainable innovation is a crucial link in aligning environmental regulation with enterprise productivity growth. Given that innovation activities are characterized by long cycles, high investment, and high risk, the intensity of a firm's innovation efforts depends on managerial assessments of risk and the expected benefits of innovation. At the same time, sustainable innovation as a special type of innovation exhibits dual externality effects, which are primarily influenced by stakeholders and external institutional pressures. Nevertheless, internal factors, such as corporate governance and business strategy, remain equally important.

Sustainable innovation is transitioning from a voluntary stance to a strategic necessity for market entry. Effective management will improve a firm's competitiveness and unlock business opportunities in pursuit of sustainable and low-carbon development. Based on the discussion in this chapter, the policy orientation at a practical level appears relatively clear. First, in the current era of emissions reduction, enterprises must meet decarbonization demands and promote environmentally friendly technological innovations. Accordingly, it is necessary to renew company strategies and restructure organizational systems.

Simultaneously, a change is needed in managerial perceptions, expectations, and attitudes toward risk in order to enable effective implementation of sustainable innovation strategies. In addition, attention should be paid to the development of a robust intellectual property system, financial support in the form of government subsidies and tax incentives, and the creation of innovation platforms and similar mechanisms to promote the spread of innovation. In terms of external effects, it is crucial to recognize mechanisms for stakeholder cost–benefit sharing and to balance the interests of all parties involved.

Sustainable innovations are difficult to implement, as social, economic, and technological systems remain locked into traditional technological pathways. Therefore, overcoming this lock-in requires both internal and external efforts, along with an internal driver that supports the external enabler, to break free from the traditional path, shift the technological trajectory, and create a spiral of sustainable innovation development.

The third chapter examines the evolution of corporate finance management, going beyond the traditional framework of profit and cost optimization. It emphasizes that digitization, sustainable development, and innovative approaches to risk management, as well as taking into account the psychology of financial decisions, are redefining the standards of operation in the area of corporate finance. Companies that can flexibly adapt to these trends increase their resilience, attractiveness to investors, and ability to build value in a dynamic economic environment.

Corporate financial management is a comprehensive process that includes planning, organizing, directing, and controlling financial flows in an organization. Effective investment and financial decisions, made on the basis of risk analysis, the time value of money, and the expected rate of return, contribute to the implementation of the company's strategic goal, which is to maximize its market value.

In a volatile and unpredictable economic environment, financial management requires not only knowledge of accounting and finance principles but also the ability to adapt to dynamically changing market conditions.

The more common appearance of humanoid robots in enterprise environments changes the way in which organizations across sectors conceptualize labor, service, and human–machine collaboration. From hospitality and healthcare to gastronomy and corporate management, humanoid robots are increasingly being deployed to perform a wide range of functions—from customer-facing tasks and logistical support to cognitive rehabilitation and executive decision-making. Their design, which mirrors human form and communicative behavior, makes them especially suitable for roles requiring social interaction, responsiveness, and adaptive engagement. However, their expanding presence raises critical questions about efficiency, user acceptance, and the broader societal implications of automation.

Chapter 4 underlines the need for a human-centric and ethically grounded approach to humanoid robot implementation. While robots offer tangible benefits such as improved consistency, cost reduction, and the ability to fill labor gaps, their usage must be carefully balanced with considerations of human oversight, algorithmic fairness, emotional intelligence, and regulatory compliance. Ethical concerns, ranging from data privacy and AI bias to transparency and accountability, must be addressed within robust frameworks such as the EU AI Act and GDPR, especially in high-risk contexts like healthcare and autonomous decision-making. Ultimately, humanoid robots should be viewed not as replacements for human workers, but as tools that can augment human capabilities, support well-being, and foster innovation—provided that their deployment aligns with organizational values, legal standards, and societal expectations.

Moreover, the chapter reveals that successful employment of humanoid robots depends not only on technological advancement but also on contextual sensitivity, including sector-specific needs, cultural attitudes, and stakeholder trust. Acceptance is influenced by perceptions of anthropomorphism, ethical transparency, and the clarity of robot functions. Managers, policymakers, and designers must, therefore, engage in ongoing dialogue with users and regulators to ensure that implementation strategies reflect both operational objectives and human values. This includes preparing for the emotional, psychological, and social dimensions of human–robot interaction, which vary across industries and user groups.

In conclusion, the rise of humanoid robots in enterprises is not merely a technological phenomenon—it is a socio-technical transformation that challenges conventional boundaries between human and machine roles. To handle this change responsibly, organizations must adopt interdisciplinary approaches that combine technological competence with ethical foresight, legal awareness, and a commitment to inclusive design. Humanoid robots have the potential to enrich enterprise operations and public services, but only if their development and deployment remain anchored in principles of respect, accountability, and human dignity.

In the face of a dynamically changing economic landscape, shaped by technological progress and globalization, companies are faced with the need to constantly adapt and look for new paths of development. For this reason, and on the basis of the chapters submitted, the following general conclusions can be formulated:

1. Effective adaptation to digital transformation through the implementation of innovative management models is crucial for the survival and development of modern organizations.
2. Sustainable innovation is evolving from voluntary action to a strategic imperative, requiring a holistic approach that combines internal and external factors.

3. Modern financial management goes beyond traditional calculations to become a comprehensive strategic function that must take into account digitalization, sustainability, and the psychological aspects of decision-making.
4. The deployment of humanoid robots in businesses represents a complex socio-technical transformation that requires a prioritized ethical and human-centric approach to realize their full potential without compromising human dignity and values.

To conclude, the reflections presented across the four chapters emphasize that current developments in business are not only technological, but also organizational, financial, and ethical. Companies are facing practical questions about how to adjust their structures, strategies, and expectations in response to digital tools, sustainability demands, and the presence of intelligent machines. The examples discussed show that progress requires more than the simple adoption of devices or platforms; it requires a consistent, responsible approach to how decisions are made, how goals are set, and how people are involved in the process.

Innovation, sustainability, finance, and robotics may seem like separate areas, but in practice, they are closely connected. Each decision in one domain has consequences in others. For example, choosing to introduce a humanoid robot into the workplace is not only a technical step—it affects the company's culture, financial planning, human resources, and external reputation. Similarly, implementing sustainable practices cannot be reduced to marketing slogans; it requires long-term planning, rethinking supply chains, and accepting new forms of risk.

The conclusions reached in this book point to a broader observation: Companies that wish to remain effective must build strategies based on clarity, responsibility, and respect for the people involved, both within and outside the organization. Progress is not automatic. It depends on deliberate actions, careful evaluation, and the ability to combine efficiency with fairness. Business management today is as much about understanding technology as it is about making thoughtful and ethically sound choices.

# Index

Pages in *italics* refer to figures and pages in **bold** refer to tables, and pages followed by n refer to notes.

For Product Safety Concerns and Information please contact our EU representative GPSR@taylorandfrancis.com Taylor & Francis Verlag GmbH, Kaufingerstraße 24, 80331 München, Germany